QUICK! HOW DO YOU DIAL 9·1·1?

Lifelines and Laughlines of a Firefighter Paramedic

RANDY NICKERSON

TATTERSALL PUBLISHING
DENTON, TEXAS

Tattersall Publishing
P.O. Box 308194
Denton, Texas 76203-8194
www.tattersallpub.com

Printed in the United States of America

10   09   08   07   010   2   3   4

The stories related in this book are based on true incidents. Names, places, and dates have been omitted or altered to protect the privacy of the individuals involved. Any other similarity to actual events or locales or persons, living or dead, is entirely coincidental.

Front cover photo by Jonathan Reynolds
Back cover photos by Kerri Burnside

Library of Congress Control Number: 2001135529
ISBN-10: 0-9679775-9-2
ISBN-13: 978-0-9679775-9-1

Cataloging-in-Publication Data:

Nickerson, Randy (1953-)
    Quick! How do you dial 9.1.1?; lifelines and laughlines of a firefighter paramedic.
    Summary: Describes events in the life of a firefighter and paramedic with the Denton Fire Department, Denton, Texas.
    1. Allied health personnel. 2. Fire fighting.
I. Title.
2001   610.69   2001135529
ISBN 0-9679775-9-2 (ppbk)

ACKNOWLEDGEMENTS

I WOULD LIKE TO THANK MY WIFE, AVA, AND OUR TWO wonderful sons, Joel and Jordan. Without their love, support and forgiveness, I would be lost.

Mrs. Linda Coolen inspired me to write my first essay. She taught me and encouraged me. She was instrumental in getting me started on this journey into the land of the printed word.

Crystal Wood at Tattersall Publishing made this possible by taking a chance on me. She has taken me from being just another guy who types to being a published author.

For the persistent encouragement Pat Coate gave me, once she recognized the genius within me.

To the Denton Fire Department: This little collection of essays says it all about the DFD and what we have meant to each other.

To the City of Denton, Texas, for paying me well for something so fun.

To all the people I have worked with. They all had a part in this adventure. It's been fun, guys and girls.

This book is dedicated to
DR. GEORGE CHRISTY.
Thank you, sir, for your inspiration
and your friendship over the years.

PREFACE

ALL THE INCIDENTS IN THIS BOOK ACTUALLY TOOK place. I was involved in each. Some happened years ago, some recently. They are all told in the way I remember them. I only wrote about those that I have sufficient recall to be comfortable saying that the underlying theme of my portrayal is accurate. I did not use the names of anyone I work with; that way, no one is embarrassed, and I get to be the center of attention in each story.

I did not think to record the exact dates and times of each incident, so I just made those up. The addresses are fictional, too, but the rest is true. All true.

A STAR IS BORN

WORKING FOR A FIRE DEPARTMENT IS THE PERFECT job. We work one day, then take off two. What can be sexier than to be on the front page of a three-page newspaper, all sweaty, with black soot all over your face, and snot in your mustache? We get lots of opportunities to help people who are having a less than optimal day. Most of them appreciate it. Some even tell us so. It is a glamorous job.

What we call work is, for the most part, a lot of sitting around, waiting for some great catastrophe to strike. When the world comes unglued, we are thrust onto center stage. That is what we train for. That is what we live for. We don't actually wish harm on people, but if things are going to happen, we want them to happen while we are on duty. We want the unavoidable fires to erupt on our watch. It is a fact of life that people are going to get hurt and die. Since it is going to happen, let it happen near us. Sound sick? Absolutely.

We rehearse often for opening night of the big play. We train, study, sweat, and train some more. The curtain goes up and what do we do? We forget our lines. Being action-oriented guys, however, that never slows us down. We stutter, look around, and think of something else to do. Many times, all we have to do is change props. That's one thing we always hold near: Hoses, axes, flashlights, pry bars, poles with hooks on the ends—props. We never get out of our vehicle without something in at least one hand.

Giving up is not an option for us. We either put the fire out, or stay until it goes out by itself, and then sweep away the ashes. There is an old expression in the fire service: "Well, at least we saved the lot."

When I began my career as a professional firefighter, our town had about 58,000 permanent residents. We had about 25,000 more young college students who swarmed two campuses each spring and fall. Over the years the numbers have grown exponentially. Our operation has grown with the population. The equipment we use has continued to advance technologically, and we have stumbled along with it.

Lots of these people have accidents: vehicle collisions, encounters with industrial equipment, trips and falls. Many get sick, have heart attacks, appendicitis, tummy aches, hangovers, overdoses. At such times we are the cavalry. We are also the only game in town. Take your pick of dry cleaners, but if your house catches on fire, you are gonna call us.

THE ADVENTURE BEGINS

I DON'T THINK IT WAS SO MUCH THAT I ALWAYS WANTED to be a firefighter, like you hear a lot of kids say. I think it was just meant to be. After ten years or so of looking forward to getting up and going to work, you begin to realize that you are probably where the good Lord wants you to be. Once in a while I question Him, but for the most part, I trust His judgment.

I cruised around for a while after I got out of high school. It is not meant for a kid of eighteen to know exactly how he is going to spend the rest of his life. Lucky thing, too. My first few career choices just occupied my time; I kept myself and my family fed, but that was about all. Not until I was employed by the Denton Fire Department did I actually feel like I had begun my adult life as a productive, legitimate, contributing member of society. Maybe everything I have contributed wasn't always exemplary, but then, I have never been in jail. That should count for something.

I started with a group of eleven other guys on April 2, 1979. We were all just garden variety firefighters at first. They let us get over being awestruck by the glamour of the job before they cast us, kicking and screaming, into the world of emergency medicine. All firefighters in our department were required to be certified as EMTs (emergency medical technicians). Since our department also handled the ambulance service, several of us had to go on to become paramedics. This is the pinnacle of life-saving expertise outside the confines of a hospital. But first I had to learn how to be a firefighter.

We had our own in-house training academy. We were going to learn to conquer any adversity as well as to quell any conflagration. Well, somewhere along the way our education fell short. The rest of the world, as I see it, depends on us to have all the answers and know all the tricks. We are just a group of regular guys with incredible luck who are allowed to sleep on the job.

There is no exact science to firefighting. Oh sure, we learned lots of formulae for applying just the right amount of pressure to a water hose to get the ideal stream onto the fire. We learned about backdrafts, flashovers, and HBO. We learned of the proud traditions that fire fighters have upheld for eons. We learned to live hard, be invincible, and drink a lot at parties. Most of the time the theory works. Sometimes real life demands a bit more luck.

My first two years were spent watching the old salts. I tried to fit in, speak when spoken to, drink when handed a beer. I watched and learned. During this period I did pretty much what I was told. This was a completely new world to me and I didn't want to mess it up, in case I decided to spend the rest of my life in it.

For obvious reasons, firefighting, as an occupation, is like no other. When others are running out of a burning building, we are running in. When people are throwing up, we are right there returning the favor. To speak of a guy as a regular person we say, "He puts his pants on one leg at a time, just like the rest of us." Well, firefighters don't. They pull up both legs at once. That is the first clue that we are a bit different than most normal people.

I went in prepared for that first big inferno. I was ready for that child trapped in a burning building. I waited. Then we sat around and talked about all the ferocious monsters the old guys had fought in the past. I waited some more. One thing became evident. Buildings do not catch fire every day.

There is a lot of technical information that one must learn in order to be a top-notch firefighter. As the world becomes more complex, so does the job. We shroud ourselves in technology, but fighting fire is really a pretty basic premise. Go in, find the source of heat, and drown it with copious amounts of water.

A typical room fire, in which typical furniture and typical people's stuff is burning, may reach 1000^0F in less than fifteen minutes. When this is the case, the coolest place in a kitchen afire may be inside the oven, which is baking cookies at 375^0-400^0F. To open the oven door and stick your head in would be the equivalent to opening a refrigerator door and sticking your head in.

The fire service has experimented with several types of material in an attempt to keep the firefighter and the heat apart. At one time we wore pants that would melt and stick to your legs. Over the years, however, better fire resistant materials have been developed. We are really invincible now, and most of the hair has grown back.

Our outerwear is called bunker gear. It consists of a quilted liner, made of a fire resistant material. Between the liner and the outer shell is a rubberized vapor barrier, designed to let, and keep, moisture out. The outer coat is a very heavy, burlap-like cloth. It is soaked in the miracle fire resistant stuff that everything we wear is soaked in. Normally it has reflective tape on it in several places. I first assumed this is to make it easier to find your body in the dark if you have an unfortunate mishap. Actually, it is there in order that it will show up in the newspaper when the ubiquitous photographer takes your picture at precisely the moment that you do something really dumb.

A cloth hood, a helmet with earflaps, and a facemask that covers almost the entire front of one's head protects the well-dressed firefighter. In order for the facemask to be of any significant value, an eighteen-pound compressed air bottle assembly is strapped to one's back. It contains compressed room air. Not pure oxygen. Oxygen is a primary ingredient in promoting combustion, so we think it best not to add to the chances that we will get French-fried inside a burning building if we spring a leak.

With all the gear on, an average-sized firefighter is carrying about forty-two pounds of added weight (not counting the eight doughnuts he just had while sitting around the station). Once the coat and pants begin to soak up water, it only makes it heavier. It makes one feel about the way the Michelin Man looks.

When I and the eleven other young visionaries were hired, becoming a paramedic was not required, but it was heavily implied. The recruitment process of who goes to paramedic school is a game of psychological warfare. Those of us who are weak-willed eventually broke down and agreed to go and be trained. "Okay!

Okay! I'll go. Just don't make me watch any more of those 'Emergency' reruns."

For sixteen years I was primarily assigned to an ambulance. During much of my first five years as a paramedic I rode an ambulance with an EMT. Many times I would be the only paramedic for miles around. Now that is pressure. Everybody looks at you to have the right answers, make all the correct decisions, and save the precariously-hanging life. I did not know that the stress would be so tremendous. Being young, I was able to cope by making a number of personality adjustments. Little did I know that it would take most of my adult life to straighten out the mess I made of my psyche during those first few years of my career.

My last year on the ambulance was hard on me, my fellow firefighters, and the people who called 9-1-1. We always say that our customers are people having a really bad day. If they had known that sometimes I was so preoccupied with my own misery that I really didn't care about their problems, they might as well have just called a plumber to come help. Lucky for them I was always covered by a very capable partner and I still had most of my wits about me.

Just as I reached the breaking point, God stepped in and lifted me out of the pit of my despair and out of emergency medicine. Either I was going to promote to the next level, or make myself and everyone around me miserable. As He would have it, I became a captain. A leader. On paper, at least. That is where I am today. By virtue of being old and getting paid more, I have to make the decisions for a crew of three or four guys. Everybody gets to offer input, mostly in the form of whining, but I have the final say, as long as my boss approves.

I always dreamed about this. I always thought about what a good job I would do as a captain, and how I would do things differently. I just knew my men would love me, yet respect my judgment. I guess every leader wants to think his people will follow him into hell. My guys don't have much choice, if they want to keep their jobs. Well, I'm working on all this. Only time will tell what sort of legacy I will leave behind. I know the stories of those who have gone before me and I suspect mine will be no different.

One little glitch in this natural progression is that I am still a paramedic. I still go to classes to keep up with the latest new stuff, and to refresh my memory, because once one stops riding an ambulance it is amazing how much one can forget. This isn't exactly like riding a bicycle. I think you *can* forget how to keep your balance. This is a big fear for me, as if I couldn't look around and find plenty of other stuff to worry about.

. . .

. . . for example, our evolving American lexicon. Next time the fire engine passes by, notice whether there's a sign on it that commands you to "Dial 9-1-1" for an emergency. Next time you look at your telephone, notice whether it has a dial. Uh-huh, I thought so.

In an emergency situation when many other higher logic functions aren't working properly, do you suppose a panic-stricken person might punch three buttons on the phone and breathlessly ask, "Quick! How do you *dial* 9-1-1?"

3

A MATTER OF
LIVELIHOOD AND DEATH

ABOUT EIGHTY PERCENT OF ALL THE CALLS WE MAKE are medically related. This is something I did learn very quickly. Many people get sick, or hurt, or sick and then hurt. Buildings seldom catch fire and many times when they do, some sick person is involved. The fire department is the logical place to base the emergency medical service. We are close. We are always there. We live to help people.

Whenever we respond to a medical call or some sort of accident, we immediately become the center of attention. Just like at a fire. All eyes are on us. The difference is that without fire and smoke we do not wear facemasks. This means I have nothing to hide the fear in my eyes. I considered wearing the mask anyway, but could not think of a good excuse to explain it. Besides, it would have made me look silly.

Maybe it was just me, but I always thought that if the taxpayers were going to lay out hard-earned tax dollars for my salary, I owed them everything I could give while on duty. I was pretty good at holding an intravenous fluid bag or a flashlight and looking sympathetic, but that just did not seem like enough. I wanted to get in there and smear blood on my face.

An entry-level emergency medical technician is roughly equivalent to a reasonably competent mother. We could bandage things. Although I never did, I could have kissed it and made it better. Anything beyond that level of difficulty, and it was over our heads. It was quite a disappointment to get that EMT arm patch and realize how little more effective it made me in dealing with people in the midst of a serious medical crisis. I did everything I could to help people, but the ability to make a difference in a sick person's quality of physical well-being was up to the paramedic. As much as I wanted to help alleviate suffering, the thought of paramedic school made me nauseated.

I resisted the persistent appeals from my supervisors for about a year. It really scared me to think about all that high-tech medical stuff. I had an inflated vision of who paramedics were and the miracles they could summon with all those drugs and electrical equipment we carry in the back of the ambulance.

Finally, I became resigned to the fact that I had to go, if ever I was going to make a real difference here. Once I capitulated and turned in my request to go, my stomach was one constant knot. When the first day of school came, it was almost a sense of relief to go and get it over with.

The three of us who took leave of our senses long enough to volunteer were soon immersed in the intense, foreign material of emergency medicine. We had first-rate instructors, with some of the most prominent physicians in the United States to oversee the program, and to come in and teach some of the more technical aspects of medicine, such as electrocardiography. One of the doctors who lectured to us worked to save the life of John F. Kennedy the day he was ambushed in Dallas.

We were given a whirlwind version of emergency medicine. For six weeks we studied. We gathered bits and pieces of knowledge, not yet really forming a clear, succinct picture of how these things were supposed to work. We learned how to speed up a human heart if it is going too slow and how to slow it down if it is racing. We learned how to get it started if it stops. We spent a month going from hospital to hospital, area to area, seeing the things we had studied being applied to real human flesh and bone.

Most of the guys who had already gone through the school made it seem near impossible to pass, much less learn the material well and excel in saving peoples' lives. I had little self-confidence at the time. It seemed to me that I did a fairly good job of handling most situations that confronted me, but I was reluctant to accept the compliments and praise given by those who watched and supervised me.

The premise of paramedicine is to deliver vital actions and drugs to people inflicted suddenly with life-threatening situations. Many of these episodes involve the workings of the heart. Actually, problems related to heart attacks provided the impetus for developing the first paramedic program. The core of the education deals with heart maladies and the drugs used to counteract various interruptions in the beating heart.

One reason pre-hospital treatment has been so successful is that a reasonably trained person of average intelligence can deliver intervening treatment successfully. Not to downplay the importance of knowing what one is doing, but medicine is an inexact science. Mistakes can be made without significantly altering the effect the treatment will have on any given patient. Our area of responsibility is such that we can fairly readily recall most of what we need to know almost instantaneously, without research. By having at least one equally trained partner alongside and a capable physician always available by telephone or radio, we are able to pull off some near miracles.

Over the years the paramedic has proven him- or herself in the emergency medical community. The doctors and nurses in the emergency rooms have witnessed first-hand our skill and talent. They have come to trust us with more and more responsibility. We now truly share in the successes and failures of medicine. We even have our own television shows.

We spent our last month of training riding a real, high-profile ambulance. Each of us was assigned as the third crew member on an ambulance in a nearby metropolitan area. During this last piece of the puzzle, the picture began to focus. We began to see how it all fit together.

The guys we rode with were pretty jaded. They had been doing it for a long time. They were burning out. Being fresh out of school and full of wonder, it seemed very arrogant of them to be so rude to the patients. These people were their employers. Most of them paid their salary through taxes. I vowed never to be so callous, so indifferent to another's pain. So far I have kept my word. I may have been less than cordial at times, mostly to the obnoxious drunks, but never disrespectful.

4

WELL, IF *YOU'RE* NOT GOING TO BRAG ON ME . . .

AFTER MORE THAN TWENTY YEARS OF DOING THIS job, and watching others do it alongside me, I consider myself to be very proficient at what I do. Yes, there are those who will disagree with me. If you knew firefighters, you would know that a consensus is unheard of. Most assuredly, there are those who know more of the small details about medicine. There are those who might be quicker to recall some of the protocol we were given to follow. There is not now, nor has there ever been, anyone in this department who cares more about providing the best possible care for each patient. At times, it is difficult to maintain a professional demeanor toward the obvious abusers of the system. I did, however, try to treat every person equally well, regardless of race, creed, or odor.

I believe I have a God-given talent for relating to people, empathizing with them, and making them feel at ease with me. My skill level is such that I show a confidence that makes people feel they are in good hands, when I am helping them. I freely admit there were times when I had not a clue as to what the problem was, but at those times I maintained my composure, knew where to turn for help, and always came through the situation able to live with my performance.

We are required to accumulate a minimum amount of continuing education credits each year. The Texas Department of Health keeps a pretty close eye on us. We must periodically show our proficiency in the procedures we are going to be delivering to the citizens. We have our own instructors, and also bring in outside professionals to teach some of the really technical stuff.

Once, I had occasion to be tested on EKGs by a nurse. Often, folks from the hospitals volunteer to help out with tests and such. They have a vested interest in what we do, since we tend to deliver our problems to their back door and say, "Here! Take this! We don't know what else to do!"

I knew the nurse from a previous event. Her husband had passed out one day, and she called the ambulance. This happened to be one of those times when I was totally at a loss for a cause of the man's problems. Not to be deterred, I asked a few lame questions, performed a few simple medical undertakings, and managed to get the man to the hospital without incurring further damage to him. It seemed rather routine, at the time, and I went on with life.

On this day, the nurse noticed that I was ashen, sweaty, obviously scared witless at the prospect of being tested. I had been a paramedic for only a couple of years, and was still in the knowledge absorption period of my life. I had not yet reached the know-everything-about-everything stage. As I began to stammer, and was on the verge of weeping uncontrollably, she stopped me. Quietly, she said, "Randy, I know you can do this. Do you remember that day you came to our house? As soon as you got there, I felt a sense of calm come over me. Your confidence reassured me, and I knew you would help us. I know you can do this, now." Her words did very little to help me with the test, but I managed to stumble through, and passed the test. It was not until later, after my blood pressure had receded, that I realized just what a gift I have here. I am pretty good at this. I have made a difference in the lives of some people who were having a really bad day.

I have mentally referenced the incident involving the nurse, and her unconscious husband countless times, over the years. It reminds me that my worth is seen by other people. Many paramedics have more book knowledge, and can spout more medical minutiae, than I. Nevertheless, I would be willing to go up against anyone I have ever worked with, in an overall patient care contest. I do not base this on my own inflated ego. I can provide numerous references, if pressed to do so.

Now, having sung my own praises, I can see just what an exemplary human being I am. Even if you can't.

5

AN EDUCATION IN DESTRUCTION

MOTOR VEHICLE ACCIDENTS ARE THE MOST COMMON type of emergency that firefighters respond to. The frequency with which people collide their automobiles together is amazing. I estimate that in my twenty-plus years on the job, I have seen over four thousand wrecked vehicles. We get called to all variety of collisions. We get fender benders and we see them shredded beyond recognition (both vehicles and people).

The amount of sheet metal damage is rarely a good indicator of the damage done to the occupants. More times than not, we will arrive to find the passengers standing next to a wad of twisted metal that looks like it has been run over by a giant lawn mower, with an occasional wheel sticking out. They might have a few cuts from the broken windows. Most of the time, at least one rider will be complaining of neck pain. A human head atop a human neck is like a balloon on a string. When one goes from breakneck to zero in under two seconds, one's head is going to keep going. Thus the descriptive word, breakneck. Then there will be people severely injured, even killed, in autos that I suspect are minimally damaging to the occupants by assessing the scene as we pull up. You just cannot guess the condition of the people inside by looking at the outside of the car.

In the early years of my career, my forte turned out to be taking care of injured people, especially those in automobile accidents. Injured people. Not sick, throwing-up people. Blood did not faze me, unless it was mixed with stomach contents, and came up through the throat, and out through the mouth. People with broken arms, and legs, and ribs, and heads, and cuts and bruises, and objects sticking in their bodies: These are things I could lay hands on and actually make them better. No television evangelist can claim that with reliable proof.

Injuries are straightforward. I can spot a broken arm from across the street. Things I can see, I can treat. We bandage and wrap, splint, pamper, and sympathize with the suffering victim. We go to great lengths to make certain that people are not worse off for having been lugged to the hospital by us in a bouncing ambulance. Everybody gets a ride on a stiff, uncomfortable board, with several ill-placed seat belt straps across the front of their already hurting body. We like to make it look much worse than it actually is by packaging the person to look like they were about to be shipped out for next-day delivery.

Things were different back in the old days. I'm talking way back in the late 1900s. Seat belts were not required by law. The speed limit was seventy on the highways (which realistically translates to about seventy-eight). Drinking and driving laws were yet to become fashionable. All these factors combined made for some very mangled bodies.

Back in those carefree old days (before AIDS became a household word), getting bloody was fashionable in our line of work. The amount of blood one got on one's arms and clothes was the indicator of how good an incident was. You got extra points if you smeared some on your face. We even wore light-blue shirts, so as to contrast the bright red blood better. Rubber gloves were used only by Howie Mandel to make himself look like a chicken.

When I was a rookie, with no appreciable emergency medical training, I was just extra help. We arrived on an engine to assist the ambulance guys. We held things, looked concerned, and washed antifreeze and oil off the street. That's about all. The paramedics handled all the real technical stuff. It was fun at first, but after a few months of standing around, holding a flashlight, I began to feel so useless. I needed to earn my money.

I have evolved, adjusted, grown, and yielded to popular opinion since first beginning this journey. The years have slowly made their way past me. The job has been a series of separate, distinct events. Each episode ends before the next begins. Sometimes there are long periods between incidents. Sometimes they are divided only by a ride in a large, brightly lit, and noisy vehicle. At least I've never been the one lying down in it.

6

THE ADVENTURE BEGINS . . .
AND NOW THERE'S NO NET

September 13, 9:42 AM:

Structure fire, 1500 block of Glowingember Drive

I have been on the job for about six months. The alert tone still sends a flood of adrenaline (*epinephrine*, to us medical types) into my system. The mere prospect of fighting a real, live fire makes my mouth turn to cotton. Adding to the intensity of the moment is the fact that there are only two of us in the station. These were lean budgetary times for us.

My leader is a seasoned veteran. How do I put this politely? His twenty years' tenure can be described as one year's experience times twenty. My job will be to assist him in doing his job, and then try to remember what I am supposed to do.

The location is less than three blocks from our station. I have scant time to pull on all the bulky gear before we arrive to find flames shooting out of and around the outside of a wooden chimney atop a two-story house. Being of keen perception, I immediately size this up as unusual. The fire should be below, in the firebox. It should not be lapping at the outside of the chimney.

As my partner curses our equipment as being worthless junk, I press myself for a strategy. The next arriving engine will be at least five minutes away. It might as well be five days. Several panic-stricken people in the front yard alternate between watching our every move and watching the ever growing blaze feeding on their home. I decide to set up a ladder, which will allow me to get closer to the source of contention. A beneficial side effect of this tactic is that the people on the ground will not be able to look directly into my eyes. This way, if we succeed in stopping the fire before it burns the house completely to the ground, they will never know that I am more terrified than they. It is much easier to look like you know what you are doing once the fire is out.

I wrestle the hose up the ladder. Trying to maneuver a charged (in this case, overcharged) one-and-a-half-inch hoseline is much like what I suppose manipulating a hundred-foot stick of summer sausage would be like. It is rock-hard, and very rigid.

With the flow of water cut off at the nozzle, the line is only heavy and unwieldy. When the stream is opened, it is like hanging onto a huge, lighted bottle rocket. I have seen a grown man (let's just say that I have this friend) flipped flat on his back by opening the nozzle of a highly pressurized hoseline. The only difference is that you only get wet, and not burned, by it. And a bottle rocket is much more spectacular when shot into the air than is sprayed water. Fireworks are illegal within most cities, but spraying water is not. And, well, you get the idea. (My friend who got spanked by the hoseline told me he had never been more embarrassed in public, and it really, really hurt his pride. The bruises did not last for as long as the chiding he took from his buddies.)

By the time our compatriots arrive we have managed to right the ladder, and I am on the roof spraying water furiously at the flames. The more experienced leaders know to take the attack into the house, to the source of the fire. Within fifteen minutes we have reduced the raging flames to smoke and steam.

We discover that the construction of the fireplace is to blame. A chimney enclosed in wood must be built correctly to avoid such a disaster. This will not be the last time I see someone's home damaged by shoddy building workmanship.

I have just learned a basic tenet of firefighting: Put the water in the right place, in adequate quantity, and the fire will go out. It is that simple. There is lots of technical information dealing with the physics of fire that we have studied more than once. All manner of technique has been taught to us. No matter. Water applied to a burning house will stop the fire. In the right place, in sufficient quantity, the fire will lose every time. We can't let this get out, though, or everyone will be in the business.

7

OUT OF THE FRYING PAN

August 16, 2:20 PM
Structure fire, 300 E. Deepchar Drive

When we came on duty this morning at 8:00 it was already 78°F. Now it is about 102°F. Most of the day we have been talking about how unbearable it would be to fight a fire on a day like this. In Texas, this kind of heat is standard fare for August. We all know that. This doesn't keep us from complaining about it. During the morning we have made a few minor calls, and have gotten out just long enough to get good and sweaty, and then rushed back to the air-conditioned station, where we resume our complaining about the heat.

As we leave the station on this call, we know our luck has run out. The smoke column is impossible to miss. The amount of smoke indicates that this is no dumpster fire. We struggle to pull on the heavy gear while riding in the small, rear-facing jump seat of the engine. Arriving in front of the house, the thick, gray smoke is suffocating. I quickly go to my Battalion Chief and give him my oral resignation, but he pretends not to hear me. I guess that since I am going to have to be here anyway, at least until I can catch a ride back to the station, I might as well help out. I can think about early retirement later.

For some strange meteorological reason, the smoke is staying close to the ground. This makes it very difficult to assess what is going on, especially without an airpak on. Back in the old days—like the late twentieth century—when men were real men, we did not need protection from breathing smoke. We are firefighters. That is our job. Eat smoke until you vomit. Then get a drink of water and crawl back in.

Back to the burning building. A two-story, wood-frame house. Wood siding, peeling paint. Several college-aged kids are in the front yard, looking concerned. This tells me the house is probably rented to them. There will be lots of posters and flags hanging on the interior walls. Lots of candles, probably, even in this heat. It is a small wonder that they have made it this long without catching the place on fire.

My crewmates and I attempt to go in the front door. We can see the staircase just to the right, already engulfed in flames. We work our line in about six feet, and begin spraying the mist into the fire and smoke-filled room. It instantly becomes pitch black, as the burning material within reach of the water is cooled. The steam bath lasts about thirty seconds, then the room begins to light up again. With so much residual heat built up, the wood, cloth, and whatever else is piled up in the room reaches ignition temperature, and bursts into flame again. This is where the sufficient quantity of water comes in. You must cool the burning stuff, and keep it cool, in order to put out a fire.

Having made little headway on the first try, we back outside, so as to attack from another vantage point. With so much fire involvement inside the house, we believe that about the best we can do is find a window, poke the hose inside, and let the floods begin.

It is too risky, even for a bunch of heroes like us, to try and get up onto the roof to cut a ventilation hole. If we could do that, much of the smoke and hot gas inside the house could escape upwards. Once those obstacles are removed, the house begins to cool, visibility improves greatly, and we can go in and stomp out the fire. Without that option, we will simply try to soak what we can reach from the outside, and continue to insist on making our way inside as soon as possible.

Eventually, we begin to win the battle. We surround the big house in clumps of two or three, and squirt fiercely at the smoke. About every two minutes or so, a blast of water from some crew on the other side of the building catches me in the face. This helps cool me down, and realizing this, I try to repay the favor by aiming our line back at them. I'm sure they appreciate it.

After about forty-five minutes (which is like seven years in firefighter minutes) we are able to go inside at will. We eventually make our way to the top of the stairs. Virtually everything inside is either covered with burned charcoal, or a heavy layer of black, oily soot. Everything plastic is melted beyond recognition. Even some glass items are reduced to molten blobs. All the delicate, potted cannabis plants are wilted beyond hope.

Once the smoke clears enough to allow us to see through the burning tears, we wander through the structure looking, poking, and putting out all the tiny, hidden fires embedded within the contents. Most people can use the phrase "once the smoke clears" only figuratively. We can actually claim ownership to waiting for the smoke to clear.

One thing we do not lack, as firefighters, is tenacity. We have never had a situation where we got to a point that we had to say, "Well, ma'am, we have done about all we can do. It will just have to burn itself out. We better be going now. Sorry." No. We keep pushing, chopping, squirting, and vomiting, until the demon is defeated.

After we take control of the structure, the real work begins. We spend the next two hours ferreting out small, smoldering fires. In such a large, densely-loaded house as this, there are unlimited places for a fire to hide. We must be certain we find them all before we leave. Nothing is more embarrassing than to be called back to a fire that you claim to have just put out.

I have just witnessed a fire the size of a house. Now that I am inside that house, I am looking at a fire the size of a Cub Scout pack's wiener roast fire, and it seems to be no more than a flaring match head. I can reach in with my gloved hand, pull out the biggest burning piece, and carry it outside. Once one has encountered something of astronomical proportions, normal situations seem tiny. My, how one's perspective can change.

. . .

Similar to the advent of rubber gloves as protection against infection from blood-borne pathogens, we learned that breathing smoke so thick that you can see it collect in the nasal passages is not entirely healthy for the human lung. As part of the real men image we thought so important, we were trained to forgo the equipment available for providing breathing air through a mask. We had contests, during my training, to see who could stay inside a room filled with smoke from a bale of burning hay. Never could a man be shamed quicker than to protest such practices as unsafe. It is part of the job. Like it or sack groceries for a living.

· 8 ·

. . . AND INTO THE FIRE

November 13, 4:12 AM
Vehicle fire, 2400 S. Oilslick Road

I have not yet gotten accustomed to being jarred from a semi-sound sleep by the grating blare of the alert tone. Especially at this time of morning, it takes me several minutes to fully realize where I am and what I am doing.

The three of us arrive in the small pumper to find a minimum amount of fire, barbeque-grill-sized, near the outlet area of a fuel transport trailer. The truck tractor is parked almost at a right angle to the forty-five-foot aluminum tanker trailer. The driver had to maneuver his rig into this position to offload his 6500 gallons of gasoline into the underground storage container of the petroleum distributorship.

Still being in the fog of sleep, the volatility of the situation does not immediately occur to me. We pull alongside the trailer, about sixty feet away from the fire. The flame is concentrated on the ground below the outlet pipes, which are near the center of the trailer. I can see gasoline dripping from one nozzle, and catching fire before it reaches the ground.

As I mentioned, we are in a small pumper. It is capable of pumping only about 350 gallons of water per minute (a full-grown engine can pump up to 1500 gpm). We use it mainly for grass and trash fires. The decision to bring it, instead of our real fire truck, was made by the captain based on information received from the dispatcher at the time the call was sent out to destroy our sleeping nervous systems.

So here we are, standing next to Goliath, with a virtual garden hose for an arsenal. I know that story about David's KO punch has probably been sensationalized a bit through the many translations of the Bible, but I think I know how Slingshot Boy felt. Not that I doubt God's presence here, now, but I figure our chances of reenacting a similar victory are very slim.

Carrying on the tradition of action above all else, we pour everything we have on the pool of flame. After about two minutes of this, it appears that we may be holding our own against the slowly dripping gasoline. Not knowing anything else to do, and lacking the retreat gene, we continue our spraying.

I am about to become comfortable when things deteriorate considerably. With a quick rush of hot air, a loud, low boom, and a momentary flash, the tank seems to expand, flex a bit, and break in two at the center. The fire is blown out. I do not remember shutting the nozzle off, but when I opened my eyes, the water was no longer flowing.

The tank is split circumferentially under the belly, about half way up each side. It has broken down in the middle, and is sagging almost to the ground at that point.

The back end of the tank, which is oval, and welded in place, is expanded outward, much like an aluminum can that has been frozen, or overpressurized. The front end cap is completely gone, ripped loose at the welded joint. The cap was launched straight forward, narrowly missing the tractor, which was turned at a sharp angle to the side. We later found it, after the sun came up, about 150 yards away in an open field.

Exactly what took place here was never determined. We know that the liquid gas burned as it dripped from the tank onto the ground. We believe that once the liquid was drained almost dry, the flame ignited the vapor inside the tank. This caused the rapid expansion and explosion.

Why were we not incinerated? The tank was very near empty when the driver accidentally dropped his cigarette lighter, touching off the fire. The vapor was rich enough to explode with sufficient force to rupture the tank, but did not contain enough liquid to cause a fireball once the tank failed. If there had been liquid remaining, we would have been soaked, lit, and extra crispy within seconds. By the grace of God, we were spared.

I went back later in the day, and took pictures of the scene. Even with photographic evidence, it is hard to convey the magnitude of the explosion—the intensity of the air rushing outward, and the low rumbling sound. We drove within sixty feet of a mobile gasoline tank that was on fire. What were we thinking? We weren't. We did, in retrospect, the unthinkable. I guess we were just lucky we did not have to approach from the front. That being the case, we might have been plastered by the end cap when it went south at about 150 miles an hour.

Well, you live and learn. The key word is *live*. We were allowed to live. I guess the other key word is *learn*. Did we? I have not been intimately involved in a situation like this one since. I want to think that we would go about it a bit differently, now. I'm not sure. That ethic of action above all else dies hard. Yet another key word is *dies*. At least, not yet.

WHAT TO DO, WHAT TO DO?

July 4, 9:16 pm
Unconscious person, 1522 S. Bronchial Blvd.

I have been out of paramedic school for about two months. As is usually always the case, the older, more tired driver gladly backs away from most patient treatment once he sees that the younger, more idealistic guy can do the job. I am getting fairly comfortable in my new, powerful role as God's left-handed assistant. So far, we have not come across much of anything that has been too unpleasant or difficult to handle. I knew it was only a matter of time, though.

We arrive to find a boy about twelve, struggling, barely breathing. He looks as though he is exhausted, and I expect each gasp to be his last. His mother is by his side, and very quickly, and surprisingly calmly, tells us that her son has asthma. He has had numerous bouts in the past, but none so severe as this.

We quickly apply an oxygen mask to the young man's face, and move him to the ambulance. We have just gotten him situated in the back when our patient stops breathing. I grab the bag-valve-mask, which I have used on real people perhaps a half dozen times. As I attempt to force air into his lungs, something seems different. Never have I had to squeeze the bag so hard in order to force air through the mask and into a person's lungs. It appears the little boy's disorder has so constricted his lungs that there is no room for air to go into his chest. I insist that my partner try the bag. Maybe I am doing something wrong. Maybe I have missed something. After about three attempts, he confirms my assessment.

We rapidly assemble our equipment used for doing artificial respirations and heart compressions. The machine takes over the job I was attempting to do by hand, but with very little success, either. My partner starts an intravenous line. As the young man's heart becomes more and more starved for oxygen, it finally ceases to beat. We push the drugs designed to counteract such an event into the intravenous line, with no positive change in the boy's condition. Without oxygen, nothing in the body can survive.

The machine takes over. With this level of automation, there is not much else for us to do but sit on the bench next to the patient and watch. Here I am, watching a beautiful young life slip away as his mother sits next to me.

I must have been absent the day they taught this in paramedic school. I do not recall learning what to do in this situation. I just assumed that if we did what we were taught, the drugs and our awesome skill would rectify the situation. No one ever mentioned what to do when all efforts fail, and I have to ride in a noisy, rough, rattling ambulance with a child's mother as the child dies in front of us. I could think of but one thing to do. I put my arm around the woman's shoulders. I struggled to maintain composure as she cried softly.

We managed to get to the hospital after a seemingly interminable ride. We continued the revival attempt, now assisted by a very competent hospital staff and physician.

To no avail.

This was quite a blow to my fresh, ego-inflated view of what paramedicine is about. That's what we are here for. We intervene, and head death off at the pass. Moreover, kids are not supposed to die. We can be more or less prepared for going into the nursing homes—not that it's a cake-walk then, either, but those folks have lived a long life. This kid was twelve years old.

About two weeks later, I got a small thank-you card in the mail. After having searched my mind over and over and over for something we could have done differently, the card relieved me of that burden. It expressed the mother's and family's gratitude, but more importantly, it let me know that I did all that was necessary.

I showed that I cared. I did my best. I was there. I still have the card today. Sometimes, when things look bleak, or if I just need a lift, I take it out and read it. The events of that night come flooding back in sharp focus. More importantly, it reminds me that what we do is vital, and that there are people who are grateful for our efforts, regardless of their effectiveness.

Randy,

A very special thank you for being here fast and helping us with our son. I'm not sure you really understand how precious you all are at a time like this. I realized at the time that Andy was out of our hands but you tried. For this you have our very special thanks.

· **10** ·

AWASH IN ADVENTURE

ONE OF THE MOST ENTRENCHED TRADITIONS OF THE fire service is our long history of having clean, shiny equipment. The Beatles even sang about one in "Penny Lane." Most vehicles get washed in some form every day, whether they are dirty or not.

At one particular station, the geographical layout was such that, when we pulled the equipment out onto the entrance ramp to wash it, all the soapy water runoff spilled into and across the street. The street makes a very sharp corner directly in front of the station, so the soapy water ran across the curve.

A lot of the traffic on this street happened to be college students. Now, we all know that college kids are the world's most reckless drivers. They all drive too fast. I believe they use speed limits as suggestions. If the sign says thirty, they automatically add ten miles per hour to their speed. Seventy-mile zone, they drive eighty. This gives them a chance to practice math problems before they get to class.

One day as we rinsed the ambulance off, we heard tires screeching in the street. We turned in time to see a car sliding around the corner, sideways, with the driver (who just happened to be a college student) fighting frantically to regain control. She managed to get straightened out, and went on her way. No harm done.

We discussed at length the fact that the soap in the water would add an extra measure of slipperiness to the street. We probably should do something different, in the future, but our priorities are set. Clean equipment above all else.

Twice more we were witness to careening automobiles in front of our station. The second was much like the first. Slip, slide, spin, and continue on down the street. The third guy was not so lucky. As his van entered the corner and began to slide, the rear end crossed the center line. As fate would have it, a car was coming from the opposite direction. The left front of the car hit the van just in front of the left rear tire. The entire axle assembly was torn from beneath the van. Wreckage was strewn everywhere. We stood, mouths agape, eyes wide, scrub brushes in hand, water hose still running.

Fortunately, no one was injured. As we stood around waiting for the cops to arrive, everyone kept looking at the water. The incriminating trail still led from the driveway across the street. Amazingly enough, no one said a word to us about our practice of forming a soap slick across a major city street each day.

CALL PRESIDENT REAGAN, HE KNOWS MY CASE

September 21, 2:46 PM
Medical emergency, 1122 Cookie Factory Road

We arrive at a mobile home in one of several garden spots around town to find a young lady about twenty years old standing in the doorway. She haltingly tells us that she called because her roommate is acting strangely. She leads us around to the back yard, which, like in most mobile home parks, is a thin slice of grass between two trailers. There we find another young lady, about the same age, standing on a stack of three or four wooden pallets (the kind used to move material around with a forklift).

The girl is dressed in a white blouse and white slacks. Her eyes are closed. Her arms are crossed over her chest. She says nothing as we begin to ask her questions. Suddenly, she begins to gyrate slowly. Her shoulders and hips move in a slow rhythm, as if she is dancing to music that only she can hear.

The laws are fairly clear in defining conditions that allow us to take a person into an ambulance and to a

hospital. A person must be in imminent danger, or unconscious, for us to remove them bodily to the ambulance. This girl meets neither criterion. Dancing to silent
music in your own back yard on top of four wooden
pallets is not something you need an ambulance for.
You need an agent. When we attempt to coax her down
from her stage, she resists. She never opens her eyes,
never stops swaying.

We find out from the roommate that the dancer is a
doctoral psychology student. Ahhh. Psychology student.
That explains it. You have to study crazy to perform
crazy. She has recently been under considerable stress
in school, yet she has shown no unusual signs until today. The roommate was taking a nap and when she
awoke, she found the mute performer outside.

After considerable discussion, we cannot really come
up with a good reason to remove the girl from her own
residence. She probably could benefit from some type
of therapy, but is not really in any danger that we can
see. Perhaps if the music she hears suddenly becomes
rap music, she might have a problem. But for now...

We are about to leave when the girl begins waving
her arms, eyes still closed, as if to tell us something. We
begin a game of charades, trying to guess what she wants.
She shakes her head yes or no, and sometimes motions
with her hands. She indicates she wants to write, so we
give her a pen and paper. She writes, "Call President
Reagan. He knows my case." The writing is a bit shaky,
since she is moving and is writing with her eyes closed.
We talk aloud, trying to decipher the message. As we
get close, she acknowledges with nods. She gives us
written clues. *"Le maison blanche,"* she scribbles over

the other message. I ask tentatively, "The White House?" She touches her nose. We know now that she is home, but she just has the shutters closed.

We discuss our position with her roommate in the dancer's presence. As long as she is not a danger to herself, or unless she becomes unconscious, we will have to decline taking her to the hospital. The roommate is not thrilled, but she accepts the situation.

I guess we should have called the Capitol to see if Mr. Reagan might shed a little light on her situation. Oh, well, it's probably best we didn't. Everyone knows you can't believe anything a politician tells you.

. . .

Over the years, I have had several brushes with greatness. While doing a rotation in a nearby metropolitan hospital during paramedic school, I saw a man walk by whom I immediately recognized as a national network sports announcer. Later, I was honored to hold a basin while his wife threw up in it. In the same hospital, I started an intravenous line on the chief of police of the fourth largest city in the United States. Once, my partner and I were called to the filming location of a major motion picture. We were privileged to clean the face of the star, who was sprayed with burning gunpowder when his Hollywood gun malfunctioned. Then there was the time I worked furiously to save the life of a man who shot himself in the mouth. It was not until later that I learned the man had been instrumental in developing a large radio station in a major market. He died of his self-inflicted wound, but it was never revealed to the public that it was intentional.

· **12** ·

MERRY CHRISTMAS TO ALL

December 25, 12:42 PM

Medical emergency, 1006 Downtrodden Drive.

We work on a perpetual calendar. As is the traditional way, in most fire departments. We work for twenty-four hours, and then get off for forty-eight hours. Work Monday. Be off Tuesday and Wednesday. Work Thursday. Be off Friday and Saturday. Work Sunday...you get the idea. We have our own calendars printed up in three alternating colors. This allows us to see a year into the future, and to know if our workdays fall on holidays. If you happen to get caught on the wrong shift, you must work on Christmas Day two out of every three years. Bummer. But Christmas Day is typically pretty quiet. All is calm. All is bright. That is at least some consolation.

Those of us who are still married have invited our wives and children to come and eat lunch with us on this particular Christmas Day. We have spent most of the morning preparing a feast. Another entrenched firefighter tradition is eating. We do. Lots. Often.

As the families trickle in, we begin to tense up imperceptibly, knowing what will happen. We have not made a run all morning. You know it will happen, but still marvel that it can occur with such "Old Faithful" precision.

We have almost finished loading up our plates when it happens. The alarm goes off. We grouse all the way to the ambulance, feeling so sorry for ourselves. How could someone inconvenience us on such an occasion as this? So what if we get paid well? So what if we spend seventy percent of our on-duty hours either sitting around, watching television, talking, complaining, eating, or sleeping? This guy had better really need an ambulance. He had better be dying, or we will refuse transport so fast, his head will spin.

We storm through the door of the room at the Budgetless Inn to find a startled, naked girl, about twenty or so, huddling beneath a blanket that has not been washed in more than a few days. A quick survey of the room paints a less than cheerful picture. Her belongings are crumpled together in a small backpack. Her shoes look like they have been many miles, as does her face. The girl tells us that she has been hitchhiking for six days, and decided to use the last of her money for a room, it being Christmas, and all. She began getting sick at her stomach early this morning, and vomited twice before calling 9-1-1. She has not eaten today.

The scathing lecture we had prepared on the way seems a bit inappropriate now. We are at work doing what we love to do and here is an unfortunate person who is alone, dirty, and sick. Thinking that her physical problem is not really something that requires an ambulance, we nevertheless offer to take her to the hospital. At least she will get something to eat there. We take her to the emergency room, and ride quietly back to our families and our huge meal.

We have led such sheltered lives. When I see firefighters sitting around, complaining about being underpaid, it saddens me. We have been given everything we need in this world, with relatively little adversity, and yet we are never satisfied.

CUT FROM A DIFFERENT CLOTH

December 29, 10:36 pm
Injured person, 2816 Buttonhook Road

We recognize the address as a large fabric, craft, and sewing center. We are going to assist a person found behind the store bleeding from injuries sustained at the hands of another. My mind drifts from the victim to the location itself.

"I'll bet you this guy is going to need stitches," I remark. My partner just rolls his eyes, much the way my wife does when I try to dazzle her with my wit.

"I'm sure he was pleating for mercy." My partner tries to ignore me. "Let me know if you get tired of me needling you. I can zip it at any time. I wonder why he just didn't bolt for the door? He's probably one of those seamy guys, anyway. Traffic is really making it difficult to thread our way through, isn't it? If this guy is a Singer, I hope his lip isn't busted. I wonder if the cops have collared the guys who did this. If they have, I hope they give them a good dressing down. I could do that, but anything I would say would likely be immaterial. I am beginning to see a pattern here."

The guy has been beaten vigorously about the face and upper torso. He is conscious (always a good sign), and seems to be fairly intact, all things considered. He probably thinks I am just a happy kind of guy, what with all the smiling as I go about tending to his injuries. He never even smiled. I guess he couldn't quite pin down what was so funny.

. . .

The man was breathless and shaking like a leaf when we arrived to take care of his wife, who had suddenly passed out. Once he saw that she was going to be all right he said, "All I could think to do was call 9-9-1."

TASTER'S CHOICE

April 6, 10:44 PM
Public service, 2266 Bipolar Way

We arrive at a very well-kept, upper-middle-class, brick home. As we approach the porch, the only clue of something amiss is a small stack of papers next to the front door. They appear to be bank statements, business papers, that sort of thing. The door is opened by a slightly-built woman, very sprightly, probably in her late seventies, with gray hair and a pleasant, round face. She is wearing a plain, straight dress, and is not wearing shoes, only nylon stockings. She is carrying a can of something, which, in the dim light, I cannot make out. Perhaps stewed tomatoes or beets, something like that.

"These crabapples have the most peculiar taste. Would you taste them, and tell me what you think?"

Now, never having tasted crabapples (that I can recall), I respectfully decline. My partner does the same. The lady seems neither deterred nor concerned, and begins to lead us through the house. She walks steadily forward, almost ignoring our presence, but continues to talk.

As we try to determine exactly what it is that we are supposed to be doing here, she talks and walks. I can just imagine what the 9-1-1 call sounded like. This sweet little old fruit-loop called and asked our dispatcher if she could send someone over to help her with her math homework. The dispatcher is thinking, "I don't have time for this. I know! I will send the ambulance guys. They won't mind."

We pass through the living room, where a radio is playing rather loudly. The music is decidedly Hispanic, with an accordion blaring in the background. "Did you know there are only two Spanish-speaking radio stations that we can get here?"

"No, ma'am. I did not know that." We continue to walk.

For about fifteen minutes we follow the lady through the house, looking for signs of physical problems, of which we can find none. She seems to be perfectly healthy for someone her age, as far as we can ascertain. She just doesn't know whether she is washing or hanging out.

"Do you know who our state attorney general is?"

"Yes, ma'am. Dan Morales."

"I am surprised. Not many people even know who our attorney general is. I think that is sad."

"Yes, ma'am."

We ask her about all the papers on the front porch, concerned that they might be important. She informs us that she put them outside so "they" would not break into her house to get them. "I don't care if they take all my money. Just leave me alone."

What should we do? The woman does not seem to be in any danger. She seems able to care for herself. The house is clean. She knows how to, and is capable of, opening cans (of crabapples), so she will not starve to death. Someone, some family member, is obviously in contact with her and taking care of financial matters, as evidenced by the papers we found. Whether she lets them into the house—well, that is her business, I guess.

She is just a couple of shingles short of a roof. We follow her around for a few minutes more, and then tell her we will be going. She hardly acknowledges our leaving, much as she did our arrival. We can stay, or we can go. Makes no difference to her. She is off again, on her journey through uncharted rooms, in search of a good mariachi band. She is still clutching the can of crabapples.

We drive away, with a slightly puzzled look on our faces. Nothing is as clear-cut as it seems. Sometimes the best action to take is to take no action.

As we arrive back at the station, I make a mental note to pick up a can of crabapples in the morning. I want to familiarize myself with the taste. Call it continuing education. The next time this situation arises, I will be prepared.

WASTED YOUTH

July 14, 12:20 PM
Motor vehicle accident, 4700 Batoutofhell Blvd.

We arrive at the scene, which is about ten miles from town, to find the usual accompaniment of firefighters from the local volunteer department. I can make out only one obviously damaged vehicle, which looks to have rolled at least a couple of times and landed on its side, just on the edge of the interstate. As I walk toward the heaviest concentration of hand-held lights and glow-in-the-dark yellow striping, I meet a couple of volunteers whom I recognize. They don't say much, but have a queasy green tinge about their faces.

I see a person sprawled on the concrete ahead, and as I approach, it is obvious why the guys leaving were not doing so well. There is a girl, probably about eighteen, lying face down. I can see the point of impact from the stains. Her direction of travel is delineated by the stream of blood and clear fluid that came from the top of her head when she impacted the pavement. A piece of her skull, about four inches around, and a large portion of her young brain are lying about eight feet out in front of her body. About three feet farther down the road is a beer can, with a trail of foamy liquid leading to it.

The vehicle the girl was driving is lying on its side. It looks to have rolled over at least twice. The girl's friend, who was a passenger in her vehicle, is sitting next to it, looking straight ahead. She sometimes blinks when asked a question, but other than that, makes no effort to communicate with us. She does not appear to be seriously injured, with just the usual abrasions and small lacerations from the shattered glass.

The urgency within the first reports prompted the dispatcher to send two ambulances on the initial call. We help place the girl with minor injuries into the second ambulance. We will stay and assist the volunteer department with clearing the scene.

I sometimes think about the girl who survived. Does she still have the vivid images of that night that I have? Does she still remember her friend, one minute alive, the next . . . Does she hear the sounds of the crash, the screams of her friend? Did she go over to where her friend was lying? How did this affect her life? How has it affected mine?

Before going back into service, we walk around the scene, burning certain images into our minds forever. I can see the shattered young body still today. I can see the beer can, lying there in a collinear line from the point of impact with the other fragments of the girl's life. It seems to be an all-too-sad reminder that drinking and driving just do not go together.

Having been through my own childhood adventures, I can see how things might have been much different for me. My head is no more shatterproof than hers. I realize how lucky I am, getting to see such pointless waste.

. . .

Then there was the lady who called because she was having trouble breathing. She said she believed she had something lodged in her sarcophagus. I always believed that once one got to the point of having one's own sarcophagus, it was way beyond our doing anything to help. Nevertheless, we treated her respectfully, efficiently, professionally, and took care to see that she lived to misuse other words in the future.

16

DADDY, YOU'RE FUNNY!

August 3, 3:15 PM
Injured person, 1414 Gymnastic Way

On a tree-lined street in a middle-class neighborhood, we find a cute little girl, about eight, waiting on the curb. She tells us that her dad is "stuck" in the back yard. Her mom has gone shopping. Upon rounding the corner of the house, I see a round trampoline with a metal frame, springs around the perimeter, and no protective cover over the springs.

On the far side, I see a body's legs, bent at the knee, with the toes sticking up under the fabric. The figure looks like a trapeze artist hanging upside down on a swing. I walk around the trampoline and see the rest of the body hanging inverted. The back of his head is touching the soft ground below. His neck is bent to the point where his chin is almost touching his chest.

He looks exhausted. I would be too, were I in his predicament. He is in an embarrassing position. Much like a turtle on its back, he is ever so close, only not quite able, to freeing himself. Being the consummate professionals always, we only briefly make light of his

situation. Once we are satisfied that his neck is not injured we help him disentangle his limbs from the con-
traption. Once he is able to stand up, and unwind some
of the kinks that have developed over the past thirty
minutes, he says that he feels fine.

Never would I have imagined that a person could become ensnared in this manner, nor have I seen or even
heard of it since. To be invited into someone's backyard,
and to see this, for me, is almost too good to be true. It's
not a big thing, but this is the kind of stuff we get paid for.
It's like getting to go to the circus for free every day.

17

ROUTINELY ADVENTUROUS WORK

ONE OF THE MOST FRUSTRATING ASPECTS OF EMER-
gency service has been trying to find the right
addresses. Something odd overtakes my brain when a
blaring tone goes off. I jump into a large vehicle, turn on
lots of flashing lights, and crank up a siren so loud that
you cannot hear the guy sitting next to you. I couldn't
find my own house when I am driving an ambulance
with the lights and siren going.

Imagine what it's like to drive past people standing
expectantly in their yards, with the siren screaming as
we go by. They see us turn at the next corner, go back
by in the opposite direction one block over, and then
come blasting back to the right location, which is three
houses back from where they are standing. We then
bound out, lug all of our equipment into the house, and
expect the people who called to believe that we are highly
trained and skilled professionals.

It is a combination of senses and reactions. Adrenaline flows just thinking about what will be found at the
end of the trip. Making all that noise, I know almost
every person who hears the siren will stop and look. All
eyes are on us. It is a very intense experience.

Rural addresses are always treacherous, especially in areas where the city hasn't yet assigned a street address corresponding with their Rural Free Delivery address. Hoping to be helpful, they describe the site you're looking for. Then it turns out that every mobile home in the park is brown with yellow trim, and a majority have a red pickup parked out front. It seems like a good idea to turn on your porch light so we can find your house at night. The problem is, everyone else on your street will have their light on, also. If they didn't already, they will turn it on when they hear the siren, just to see what is going on.

It is very disconcerting to spend precious time looking for a house while knowing someone may be dying there. We have points against us right off the top. We quickly recover, though, and deliver our best every time. It is just that our best might vary a little from time to time, due to all the factors we have to deal with before we arrive.

18

A VICTIM OF CIRCUMSTANCE
AND MACHINERY

September 4, 2:38 PM
Injured person, 2400 Bear Trap Drive

We arrive at a large discount store. An employee directs us to the back of the building and into a secluded hallway near an employee lounge area. In a small alcove there are several vending machines. Here we find a young boy, about ten, kneeling in front of one of the large machines. It is the type with a glass front, containing assorted snacks stacked inside large corkscrews. When a number is selected, the purchase is cranked to the end of its row and falls into the tray at the bottom. As an outside door is pushed inward to retrieve the snack, another flap simultaneously swings up to prohibit someone from reaching up and grabbing additional snacks.

Our little patient thought he could beat the system. He thought he could snake his tiny arm up far enough to snare a treat. Obviously, the people who designed the machine planned for such a contingency. Even a ten-year-old boy's arm is too large to negotiate the angles necessary to reach the food. He is now hopelessly stuck.

A bit like Chinese handcuffs, the harder he struggled, the tighter the hold became. He offers little explanation, and doesn't seem to be very remorseful, either.

We apply a generous coat of K-Y jelly to his skin and are then able to force the plastic flaps enough to free the delinquent. His parents are nowhere to be found. After we determine that he has no serious injuries, other than a bit of bruising to what little pride he might have, we leave him with the store employees and the local police, who have now arrived.

19

AN ANGEL LOSES ITS WINGS

January 26, 11:06 AM
Injured person, 305 Slash Circle

It seems a little early for a bar fight, but by now, there is not much that surprises me. If it does, I make extensive mental notes and vow never to be surprised by it again.

As we enter the shabby, dimly-lit club, we are led around several pool tables to the back of the room. Only a handful of patrons sit around the place. Smoking and drinking seem to be the order of the day. No one appears to be too concerned about what is going on.

Beside the last pool table we find a large man lying flat on his back. He is wearing a goose-down jacket, and it is covered with blood. Someone has placed several paper towels across his throat. We later decided that whoever put them on his neck did not care about stopping the flow, but rather just did not want to have to look at the gaping wound and all the blood.

When I remove them, I am somewhat surprised at the extent of the laceration. I quickly get over that. This is going to require some fairly rapid intervention. I see why the sight was disrupting the locals' beer drinking—the cut extends from just below his right jaw, downward, across his throat, and to within an inch of his left clavicle. It is deep.

The man is semi-conscious, mumbling, groaning, and incoherent. Once we have attached the LifePak (EKG monitor) to his chest, we see that his heart is beating furiously. The pulse at his wrist is weak. He has obviously lost most of his blood and is barely alive. Needing to work expeditiously to replace the blood before his pump runs dry, we do what we always do. We whip out the ever-present heavy-duty scissors (the kind that will cut a penny in half) and go to work on the coat and shirt.

I never really stopped to think what the inside of a goose-down coat looks like. I guess I did not visualize what down actually is: feathers. Lots and lots of tiny, white, weightless feathers. Combine these with copious amounts of red, sticky blood, and, well, you get the idea. It was the unintentional equivalent of tarring and feathering the guy. Were the man's physical condition not so serious, I would have stopped and laughed at the sight. Being concerned for his well-being, I laughed as I worked.

The intravenous Ringer's Lactate fluid did the trick. It restored his circulatory system to an adequate level, enabling his heart to slow down. His blood pressure rose to a tolerable level once we stopped the severe bleeding. Miraculously, the major vessels along the sides of the neck were not cut. We were able to control the bleeding with lots of gauze dressings and direct pressure.

By the time we arrived at the hospital, probably eighteen minutes after we were called, the man was talking to us. He was still slightly confused, as one might imagine, but he was alive. He was also covered with tiny white feathers, but did not seem to mind.

Imagine being in a heavy mental fog, and then waking up with an indescribable pain in your throat and covered with feathers. You might think you had been attacked by a giant chicken. If you survived, it would be a great story to tell next time you were at the pool hall.

20

LIQUID ADVENTURES

THE ABSOLUTE WORST THING ABOUT WORKING IN THE EMS business is the vomit. I always try to maintain a professional demeanor in the face of abuse, but if you vomit on me, I am going to vomit back. I can tolerate blood without blinking. I might have gotten queasy a few times in situations where a body was disfigured, dismembered, or worse, but I never lost control of my cardiac sphincter because of it.

I am not sure if it is the smell that sets off the retaliation reflex. Partially digested stuff has its own distinctive odor. It could be the texture. Chunks set in liquid. Sticky goo. Usually always some color of grayish orange, with flecks of brownish black. I guess it might be a combination of senses insulted all at one time.

Through the years, the name has changed. The action has remained pretty much the same—gross. Little kids spit up. Others oop up. One lady told us she had been vomicking for two hours. When you begin to mature you throw up, or vomit. In coarser circles, you puke. More recently, people have begun to spew, blow chunks, hurl, purge, blow chow, or toss cookies. When college kids drink too much, they pull the trigger. I had a track coach during high school who referred to it as pitching up your chili.

If a drug overdose (by mouth) was suspected, we had to try and save any effluent we encountered between the house and the hospital. For a long time, we carried a drug designed to make a person evacuate the contents of their stomach. If such was indicated, we would wait until we could see the hospital up ahead, and then hurriedly give the medicine. This was sort of like lighting the fuse on a stick of dynamite while running towards your target. You just hoped you got there in time. Once we were inside the emergency room, we would usually help strain through the soup, looking for any pill fragments that might be in it. That is why drug companies make pills in such bright colors—it makes them easier to see amongst that brown gravy.

About the worst thing to meet on the way back up is Fritos and chili. Ice cream and anything is particularly disgusting. I once saw a section of wiener at least an inch long—some people just do not chew their food. Scrambled eggs change form less than anything, and are easily recognizable with pieces of bacon mixed in.

When the going gets tough, the tough throw up. It's just part of the job.

21

I DOUBLE-DOG DARE YA!

January 24, 10:46 AM
Motor vehicle accident, 1900 Senseless Blvd.

From about a block away we can see the form lying beside the road. The sun is out, the roads are clear and dry. About three or four inches of slushy snow remain on the grass. For about the first two minutes after we arrive we focus entirely on the man, probably thirty-five, who is crumpled there. He has no pulse, his limbs are twisted into positions impossible to achieve unless bones are broken, and his eyes are open with the death stare I have begun to become accustomed to seeing much too often. There is nothing we can do for him.

As we slowly accept the fact that we cannot help him, we go into investigator mode. How did this happen? Why? I guess it is part of the process of rationalization to want to know why people die, and why we cannot prevent it.

The snow clearly shows the tracks where they begin, about fifty feet back up the street. Just as quickly as the vehicle left the roadway, it swerved back onto the pavement, and is nowhere in sight. The man was obviously struck from behind, so he had little warning, depending on how fast the vehicle was traveling.

By now the cops are swarming, and have put out the word for their buddies to be looking for a damaged vehicle, possibly with body parts hanging off of it. We stay on the scene for several minutes, tagging along while they investigate, offering our input as necessary. One last time, I go over to the man's body. It is a common curse to fear that we might have missed something, and the person might accidentally, possibly, by some act of God, still be alive.

As I crouch near him, I notice the watch he is wearing. When I graduated from paramedic school, my beautiful wife bought me a rather expensive watch. I am wearing it this day, as I do every day. It is identical to the dead guy's. Of course, I knew my watch was not an original, but this is the first time I have seen a dead man wearing one like it. Being one to always try and read something into everything, this bothers me. Someday, I know I will be dead, and I will likely be wearing my watch when it happens, but this is like some occult sign from God. What does it mean? What does anything in this job mean?

Later in the day, one of the cops stops by the station to fill us in. Three young men pulled up next to a beer truck making a delivery a few blocks away from the scene. One jumped out and grabbed an armload. As they drove away, someone got the license number from their pick-up truck. They were making their getaway, enjoying their plunder, when they approached the unaware pedestrian from behind.

Within thirty minutes of the incident, they were apprehended. The driver swore that the outside passenger reached over and grabbed the wheel, causing him to swerve. The passenger did not aggressively deny the allegation.

The driver and passenger are still in jail (as they should be). The kid riding in the middle got off easy. He only has to live with the memory that he took part in killing a man. I hope he saw the man's eyes, just before they hit him.

.   .   .

What are the most often-spoken last words?

"Hey, y'all, watch this!"

WORKIN' FOR THE MAN
EVER' NIGHT AND DAY

March 13, 7:48 AM
Just another day at the office.

I arrive at work. The off-going shift is transitioning from sleep to drinking coffee, and preparing to go their own ways. I find today's newspaper, scan the front page, then dig out the business section. For about the first thirty minutes or so, we talk. We discuss equipment problems, and they share tidbits of the past twenty-four hours' adventures. I prepare mentally for the day ahead. Typically, I will take two Tylenol about this time. I can feel the tension creeping up the muscles in the sides of my neck. It is an unconscious reaction to the stress of not knowing what might happen.

I spend about an hour checking the oil, measuring the air pressure in the tires, looking, pulling on belts and pushing buttons. With equipment that is normally used only under extreme conditions, we must give a lot of attention to its upkeep. Once the initial check is done, and my partner has completed his check of all the life-saving stuff in the back, we wash the outside. Being a compulsive person, I am much more comfortable in a clean machine. I always thought that if I, or my family, got picked up in an ambulance, I would want it to be as clean as possible. Inside and out.

On this day, we do not cause any traffic mishaps with the soapy water. The whole process takes two hours, give or take. Twenty-four hours is a long time, so we have learned to pace ourselves in everything we do.

About mid-morning, it begins to get warm and we all migrate back into the air-conditioned living quarters of the station. With no special duties to tend on this particular day, we talk, read the rest of the newspaper (in excruciating detail), and begin to plan lunch.

After a heavy meal, the morning's rigorous pace takes its toll. A *siesta* is in order. We believe that because there is the possibility we might not get to sleep tonight, we should catch a nap whenever time allows. Besides, having not done anything all morning, the odds against us mount with each passing hour.

Following a decent rest, it is time to man the sofa for a while longer. Before you know it, the evening news is on, and a staple of all fire station life begins: for the next seven hours we argue about what to watch. The power lies with whomever is in possession of the remote control. Still, no calls.

Around midnight, I decide to go to bed. Not that I am really sleepy. I have done nothing but sit around, talk, and watch television for the past sixteen hours. Sleep comes eventually, though sometimes, when I get up the next morning, I swear that I have been awake all night. Something inside my head is always listening, waiting for that terrible noise that signifies that it is time to earn my money.

But not on this night. One shift out of about fifteen, we do absolutely nothing. We never left the station. I spent twenty-four hours on alert, and now, as my shift ends, I feel a perceptible difference in the muscles of my neck. No headache. I am free for two days. I actually look forward to coming back, and doing it all over, though. Some days are like this.

This is a great job.

· **23** ·

A CHANGE OF PLANS

July 3, 7:36 AM
Motor vehicle accident, 612 Carnage Hwy.

After a night sprinkled with routine sick people and a couple of drunks, I am ready to go home. Or at least leave the station. I will probably go to my part-time job as a carpenter.

Instead, I get caught on one last call. We arrive to find two automobiles—big, heavy automobiles, which have hit almost directly head-on. I, along with one of the engine crew members, go to the car nearest. Damage is severe to both vehicles, with the engine compartment pushed almost back to the windshield on one.

Still in the front seat are a man and a woman. Both look to be in their mid-sixties. The man has his eyes closed. He is not moving. The lady's eyes are open, and it is obvious that she is dead. She has the stare. About an inch-long trickle of blood is visible on the corner of her mouth, but has already dried. I search thoroughly for visible clues to why she is not living, but can find none. The lack of blood and bruising lead me to believe that her heart stopped almost immediately following the impact.

I check the man's carotid pulse. His neck is cool. There is no blood movement through his circulatory system. He also is dead. I go through the same process of checking for apparent external injuries, but find few. There are no legitimately fatal wounds to be found on the man.

It is difficult for me to accept that two persons are dead here. For now, I recognize that fact, and move on. We go around the wreckage to where the driver of the other vehicle is lying flat on the ground.

Subconsciously, I begin to visualize what has happened. We are in the middle of a divided, four-lane freeway. The dead husband and wife are headed in the right direction on their side of the road. About fifty yards in front of their car is an exit ramp. The other driver was driving the wrong way up the service road, and entered the ramp going the wrong way. It happens to be on a small rise, which prevented the man and woman from seeing the oncoming vehicle in time to avoid it.

The kid in the other car is probably twenty years old. He is bloody, mostly from his nose and cuts on his face and upper body. He is unconscious and is breathing slowly and deeply. I can smell the familiar odor of alcohol about him. Almost automatically, I insert a tube down his nose. This relieves the distress he was having breathing, and his condition improves noticeably. He is still unconscious, but begins to move around purposefully. From where I am standing, he appears to be lucky that he is not aware of what is going on. He does not have to see the two people he has just killed.

We take all the appropriate precautions to prevent further damage to the kid, and place him in the ambulance. As my partner takes care of him, I just have to go back once more, and make sure the two deceased have not come back to life, or worse, were not really dead, and I just missed the pulse when I was there before. As I suspect, their condition has not changed. I only notice how little outward evidence there is that they should not still be alive.

Professionalism is required at times like these. The situation is fairly evident, and is later confirmed through the police report. A kid has been out drinking all night. He is trying to get home before the sun comes up. A couple, who are going on their first vacation since retiring, drive unwittingly into his path. They pay with their lives. He is beat up, but will survive without permanent damage. His unconsciousness turns out to be more of a side effect of the alcohol than any type of physical damage from the impact.

We have expended all of our energy on his behalf. It does not seem fair, or rational, to treat someone like this with such respect. I want to tell him what he has done, if he does not already know, but he is pretty much out of it. Lucky for him.

WHY ME, LORD?

THINGS HAVE BEEN PILING UP FOR A WHILE NOW. THE girl splattered all over the highway. All the loud-mouthed, obnoxious drunks. Now these two innocent people, killed by a stupid, drunk kid. All the everyday crap we have to put up with. Normally, I would go from the station directly to my part-time job, but I just can't do it today.

It is not something I can pinpoint, but my existence seems out of balance. I always believed that life was a process of growth, maturity, and then one day reaching a zenith of perfect order, and peace within the world. My long-time best friend, who started to work the same day I did, has a different view on this. His view is that one's life is in constant turmoil and crumbling like a sand castle. Entropy makes perfection unreachable. The best we can do is to continually strive to patch up our individual sand castles and struggle to keep them from falling completely apart. Today, I agree with him.

Why do I have to see so much death? Why am I not able to explain to my wife, or anybody, what all this is like? The stories always seem to lose something in the translation. Maybe I just speak a language that no one else can understand.

I talk to God a lot. I figure He owes me answers. That is why Christians pray: so He will respond in that loud, booming, Hollywood voice. So that life will make sense, once He has explained everything. Perhaps some-day it *will* all make sense.

On this day, rather than go to my other job, I am sitting on the cool concrete floor beneath our carport. It is about 10:00 A.M. A pretty day. Clear, warm, not too hot, a little breeze. I am very comfortable, physically. It is one of those days that would be great for doing some-thing fun, if I just felt like it. Nothing would be fun to-day. As good as things are for me right now, my head will not accept it.

It is too early to drink. I maintain a strict moral code in this area. I never drink before 11:30 A.M. Through lots of trial and error, this has emerged as the appropriate point for the first drink of the day. Maintaining moral standards is important to me. Life is tough, so I try to do what I can to cultivate a good working relationship with God. Besides, if I drink any earlier I always get a head-ache.

As I stare at the sky, a bird suddenly flies (more like flounders) beneath the ceiling of the open carport. It bonks into the wall, falls to the floor, flaps its wings a couple of times, and within a minute, it is stone dead.

Now this must be a sign from God! I have no idea what it means, but it has to be a sign. Instead of a burn-ing bush, I get a dead bird. A sick swallow. A moribund martin. When you think about it, how many people have ever seen a bird fall to earth, and just die? Well, okay, maybe a lot, but this is the first one I have ever seen. God is air traffic control for all birds, so I know He guided this lark on its last leg here. I guess He just wanted to remind me that "His eye is on the sparrow, and I know He watches me."

I feel better now.

. . .

Once I saw a guy who had accidentally slashed his wrist on a broken window. He was afraid he had cut all the tentacles to his fingers. Since he could still wiggle all of them, I assume the tentacles were not cut. Neither were the tendons.

· 25 ·

THE SEATBELT SIGN IS NOW ON

February 23, 10:55 PM
Motor vehicle accident, 1515 Flyingblind Road

The call comes in as a possible downed airplane at the municipal airport. On the way we find out that the plane is still in the air, but having problems. The trip to the scene takes about three minutes, and by the time we arrive we have a pretty good idea of what is going on.

There are two people in the small plane. The man is flying, and his wife is handling communications on a cellular phone. On their approach to the airport, the plane suddenly lost all electrical power to the lights and gauges inside the cockpit. The engine continues to run, but the landing gear will not come down. They have a small flashlight and thus can monitor the gauges, which are still functioning. The pilot has manually lowered the wheels, but he does not think the nose wheel is locked into place. He is afraid to attempt a landing without visual confirmation that all his wheels are down. That's where we come in. We can provide lights, and eyes, and foamy water if things do not go as planned.

The phone has its own battery pack, which is salvation for them. The lady calls 9-1-1. Due to some freak of nature, or, more likely, some glitch in man's highly advanced technological design, the call is picked up by an operator in Amarillo, three hundred miles away. Being quick on her feet, and probably accustomed to dealing with such highly sophisticated electronic wizardry, that operator transfers the call to our dispatcher.

We have three engines set up in a standardized con-figuration along the runway. The equipment is positioned to reach the plane anywhere along the runway, in case it comes down wrong. Once we are assembled, we turn off all our engines in order to listen for the plane. Within a few minutes we begin to pick up the drone of the small engine. As they pass overhead in front of us, we can make out the shape of the plane in the glow of all the surrounding lights.

As the situation evolves, I become the liaison between the plane and us. Our dispatcher gives me the cellular phone number. My first few minutes on the phone are more or less a get-acquainted dialogue. Their phone's battery is growing weak. We have to constantly redial when the signal is lost and the phone hangs itself up. With only a couple of brief conversations, I feel like I know the two people circling around over our heads. It is hard to tell who is more nervous, even though I am safely on the ground.

"Just tell us what you need, and we will do every-thing we can," I reassure the wife.

"Well, I hope you guys don't get a fire call, and have to leave us," she jokes nervously.

"It's a pretty slow night. Maybe we can hang around a while. I'd like to see how this turns out, anyway," I joke nervously. "Don't worry. We are here until this is over, and you guys are on the ground."

After discussing the situation, we devise our plan of action. The pilot will make a low pass down the runway. We will use our floodlights to try and determine the position of the landing gear. If the wheels are down, all they have to do is set her on the runway, nice and easy. If they are not down, well . . . we will do something else.

His first run is a bit high, and we cannot positively say that the front wheel is down. The rear wheels look fine. We ask him to make one more pass, a bit lower, just to make sure of what we are seeing. On the second pass, it is obvious the front wheel is partially extended but not locked in place. It is tilted back about thirty degrees, or so.

By now the plane's fuel is getting low, which is good, to a certain extent, if one is going to make a crash landing—I mean, *emergency* landing. The pilot conveys his apprehension about the procedure to be followed. It has been a long time since he practiced it. My thought was, just how well can you practice landing your airplane without all the wheels down? We happen to have a pilot on one of our crews, so I suggest the two go over the planned landing. Our guy tells the pilot, "I want you to have your airspeed as low as possible, without stalling, when you come in. Use the flaps to slow it down. Just before you touch down, open both doors, and take off your seat belts. As soon as you feel it touch the ground, pull the yoke back hard, into your chest. Once you start to hit the brakes, be ready to jump, if it comes to that."

I am in the engine positioned at the midway point on the runway. It is our job to pull in behind the plane when it passes. If it does not make it to us, we can turn up the runway and meet it. If it passes by, we will be pulling up behind it by the time it stops.

We have now been here for over an hour, and the tension is pretty high. We are ready to do our job, but hope that our expertise will not be needed.

We put as much light as possible on the runway. Even then, we are unable to see the plane until it is almost directly in front of us, and going by. All three wheels are on the ground, and it appears the landing was successful. The first ground contact was likely hard enough that it knocked the nose gear into locked position. We all gather around the shaky couple and exchange hugs and handshakes. I have pumped enough adrenaline to last a week.

A few days later I received an enthusiastic letter from the pilot and his wife. They were very appreciative of our professional, yet personal attention to their situation. If you want to look at it this way, one might believe that they landed safely and did not crash because of the job we did. Nevertheless, I am very grateful that they have given me reason to continue my chosen profession. It makes me think that I am on the right track with this pursuit of excellence obsession.

. . .

Then there was the rather large, older lady whose elevator stopped just short of the top floor. When I asked her what I could do to make her more comfortable during the ride to the hospital, she matter-of-factly said, "Get Johnny Mathis to come and sing 'Chances Are' to me and I will die a happy woman."

"I'll see what I can do, Ma'am."

Later I foolishly asked the same question again. "Give me a good-lookin' man for fifteen minutes, and I'll die a happy woman."

"Sorry, Ma'am. I am on duty right now, and besides, our rules strictly forbid . . ."

OH, BABY!

August 21, 3:30 PM
Motor vehicle accident, 7900 N. Gridlock Way

"Medic 533, be enroute to an MVA, 7900 North Gridlock Way." We just happen to be cruising along after going to Central Fire Station to pick up an order of medical supplies. It is a hot day, and we need something to make us look busy, something that can be done mostly in the cab of the air-conditioned ambulance. So we cruise.

As we switch on the red and blue lights and siren, the traffic ahead begins to catch the reflection in their rear view mirrors, and most pull to the right. As we gain speed, we overtake the flow of vehicles more quickly, and often have to slow until the driver ahead looks up.

The address is about twelve miles up the interstate. For the first time in over twenty years the aging highway is being almost totally reconstructed. We know that in the vicinity of this address, traffic is restricted to one lane in each direction with a heavy concrete divider between.

About four miles from the accident we hit the backup. Obviously, traffic is stopped and likely is being rerouted onto the service road by the always-present state troopers. I press through the line as best I can, moving from outside to inside, depending on which way the drivers ahead decide to go. There is no way of knowing how a person will react to an approaching emergency vehicle. I have seen people pull across the center stripe or even into oncoming traffic rather than move to the right side of the roadway, as is proper. Left-turn lanes are especially inviting for people who have some deep-seated resentment of doing the right thing. Predictably, it will be the left turn we need to make. It is a constant challenge to arrive without causing damage to either us or the driving public.

As we come into view of the accident I see a full- sized pickup with heavy front-end damage. Next to it, there is a large farm-type tractor. It has huge rear wheels on the back, into which the truck apparently collided. It appears the tractor was on the shoulder of the one-lane road. Once we pull alongside ground zero, I can see that the frame of the dirt mover is broken completely in two near the middle. The thought flashes through my mind just how much impact it would take to break so much steel.

Our friends, the local volunteers, are already on the scene. I can see the familiar stance of two of them kneeling in the grass. They are doing CPR.

The all-too-familiar sinking feeling in my stomach grabs my attention. I do not want to do this. It almost always turns out badly. Persons who arrest (the heart stops, breathing ceases) before they reach the emergency room because of blood loss due to trauma almost never survive. Never. But we will do what has to be done. We always do. Always.

Once we emerge from our ride, the unbelievable heat, exacerbated by all the idling engines and the miles of concrete and black asphalt, hits me in the face for a brief moment. Knowing the system all too well by now, I ignore the sweat dripping into my eyes and go to work.

My partner goes directly to the CPR, and begins to initiate advanced procedures which the volunteers are neither trained nor equipped for. I make a sweeping survey of the entire scene, in order to triage all persons who might have been involved in this disaster.

I find only one other person: male, about thirty- five years old, covered with blood from his head to his knees. He is speaking Spanish, but that does not really seem relevant in this situation. In English, his speech would likely be incoherent, anyway. One skill I developed fairly quickly was the ability to recognize a word salad tossed in almost any language.

I probe the man's body with my hands (no gloves) in order to find any obviously broken bones and to try and determine the severity of his injuries as best I can. A little blood goes a long way when it is spread over a person's entire body. This makes it extremely hard to identify the origin of the blood loss. I try to reassure him in English, hoping he can understand. Even if he doesn't, it reassures me.

By now, another paramedic I know well has arrived, and comes to where I am beginning to prepare the man for placement into the ambulance. Believing the man is not in a life-threatening state, I ask my friend, along with a couple of the eager volunteers, to take over so that I may go and assist my partner with the CPR.

My associate has the life-saving treatment well under

way. There is little for me to do other than to assist in loading the lady onto a flat board, and then onto the stretcher. We then move to the ambulance, where we have a telephone, a semi-cool air conditioner, and four walls to shield us from the onlookers and any tabloid photographers who might be lurking nearby.

The lady is about the same age as the man I cared for. She is likely his wife, or the equivalent thereof, judging from her appearance. It is impossible not to notice that, lying flat on her back, her abdomen protrudes roundly upward.

My partner and I begin to discuss what he has done thus far, and what we both see. I then call the hospital where we intend to go and prepare them for what they can expect in about fifteen minutes. I discuss our dilemma with the emergency room doctor, who is very helpful in remembering any little nuances we may have overlooked in our hurricane-like treatment.

Due to the communication barrier with the man, along with his distressed state, we cannot confirm that our patient is pregnant. By our estimation, going purely on her physical appearance, we both guess that she is indeed in a family way, and near full term. She has the classic with-child look (a very highly technical medical term I use when I cannot think of the word *gravid*).

I relay the information to the hospital as the husband is loaded into a second ambulance, which we called as we arrived at the scene. The cardiopulmonary resuscitation continues in the cramped space of our ambulance. The doctor I speak with says little about the situation and we all agree that it is time to go. I gladly climb into the driver's seat and begin the eight-minute race back to the hospital.

When we arrive at the emergency room door, we are met by an entourage of unfamiliar hospital people. They are not regular staff here. I do recognize one man as being a doctor. I have seen his face in a newspaper advertisement.

We push the lady into the well-equipped room, which, on this day, has even more equipment laid out on a sterile tray, next to the bed. As we continue to do chest compressions, the respiratory team takes over the oxygen supply aspect of the effort.

Before I realize what is going on, the ad-campaign doctor has cut the woman's abdomen open, and is groping around inside, obviously looking for an unborn baby. After about thirty seconds he says, "This woman is not pregnant! Who said she was pregnant?" I do not bother to answer, thinking his question was more or less rhetorical. Instead, I begin to wilt into the corner, hiding behind several of the dozen or so people in the room.

I am stunned. How can she not be pregnant? I glance at my partner. He has about the same look on his face as I am sure I have on mine. He asks again, this time more loudly. "Who told us this woman was pregnant?" In a split second, I realize there is no avoiding the truth here. There is no one else to point to. I answer in an adrenaline-driven voice, equal in decibels to the irate gynecologist's. "I did! I believed she was, based on her appearance, and the way we found her." He does not respond, and there is sudden silence in the room.

The life-saving attempt is given up, and the crowd

begins to thin. I waste no time in grabbing some of our bloody equipment and retreat to the back of the ambulance under the guise of cleaning up the mass destruction we have inflicted upon it. As I sit, trying to sort out all that has happened, a familiar nurse comes out. She says, "I wouldn't feel too bad about this, Randy. He thought she was pregnant, too, or he would never have cut her open." Good point.

In the next couple of weeks, during the obligatory "tear the thing apart" period, we dissect the event with excruciating detail. We conclude that if given the opportunity to replay the event, we would do nothing differently. No further harm was done by inconveniencing the doctor. It was proper to assume that there might be a viable life inside her belly, and to go through the maneuvers we chose. So what if the doctor was embarrassed? If he had my ego, instead of enough for three people, he would be quite accustomed to being embarrassed by things.

. . .

The language barrier has been a constant problem for us. We have very few bilingual people within our ranks. So far, no one, including myself, has had enough resolution to stay with a course long enough to learn Spanish. In the absence of the proper linguistic talent, we usually all do the same thing: we talk louder. We believe that if we talk loud enough, they will eventually understand what we are trying to say.

27

YOU HAVE THE RIGHT
TO REMAIN STUPID

September 12, 2:26 PM
Unconscious person, 1813 Nimrod Blvd.

We arrive to find most of the volunteer crew standing in the front drive of a rural address. The three-story structure, which was a residence before a large lake was built nearby, now houses a bait and tackle store on the ground level. The proprietors live on the upper two floors.

The leader of the fire crew says with a big smile, "You guys aren't going to believe this. I think it will be best if we just show you."

As we climb the stairs to the top floor, the sheriff's deputy begins to provide clues as to what took place earlier today. Near the back door, they found a bedsheet with typically burglarized items piled onto it: small television, silver service, VCR, portable phone, etc. There is an old model pickup backed up outside the back door.

Believing they are about to surprise a burglar in action, the two officers drew their weapons and secreted themselves behind the nearby furniture. There they waited. And waited. About twenty minutes later, they decided something was amiss. Cautiously, they worked their way through the building, room to room, floor by floor. Finally, on the third floor, in the master bedroom, they found the culprit.

By now, we are approaching that room. As we enter, we see what the deputies saw. Sprawled on the bed, completely naked, unconscious, is the twentyish-year-old aspiring burglar. On a nightstand nearby there is an almost empty liter bottle of expensive whiskey. The puzzle pieces begin to come together.

The tape in the not-yet-stolen VCR was not the kind one rents at the local Blockhead Video Store. I guess that explains the guy's relaxed look and casual attire (or lack thereof). The most unpleasant factor is the large area of vomit around the rocket scientist's head and shoulders. He has rolled around in it, and is now wearing his lunch. Once we determine that he is breathing adequately, and his lungs do not seem to be congested by inhaled Twinkies and such, we back away. For several minutes we analyze the scene while taking his blood pressure, pulse, and breathing rate. This is a lot of fun.

We haul Einstein down the stairs, showing him meager respect, I am ashamed to say. The intravenous needle stick didn't even make him flinch. He never regained consciousness during the trip to the hospital. Or maybe he did, and realized how embarrassing a situation he had placed himself in. That is what I would do, were I a really, really, dumb crook.

Wouldn't you love to be there when his cellmate says, "So, what are you in for?"

28

LIFE GOES ON

February 16, 9:44 PM
Possible heart attack, #26 Cold Circle

The loud, obnoxious monotone jars me from a semi-conscious state. As many times as I have heard it, uncontrollable muscle contractions raise me from my seat. As the familiar voice begins to urge me toward a focus, I instinctively move toward the red and white one-ton truck.

The clattering diesel engine protests as I force it to its limits and out onto the street. As red, blue, and white strobe lights burst through the blackness, the siren bursts the night silence and my ears protest the invasion.

Thumbing through the map book, my partner finds the page quickly. Knowing the vicinity from past excursions, we discuss the area we are going into and decide the fastest route.

As I maneuver around the bewildered drivers onto the highway, once again I am reminded how diverse the reaction to flashing lights is. Some pull to the left, some to the right. The most dangerous slam on the brakes in front of you, not knowing where to go. I suggest a place for them as I squeeze past with several inches to spare.

Within five minutes we have covered the eight miles to our destination. When we pull into the driveway, the faces visible in the lights are an accurate indicator of the gravity of the situation inside. As we carry sixty pounds of equipment into the house, I begin to play out, in my mind, what we have done many times before. I know this situation will be similar, but not the same.

Our patient is a big man. My first thought is, I *hope he is still alive.* My second thought sees us straining to get him into the ambulance. His purple face and chest suggest that he is alive, but that could change very soon.

I force my mind to guide my questions and actions in the appropriate direction. Our intense, narrowly focused education leads us to the guy's heart. Although he is still talking, his heart is not doing its job effectively. Confirmed by his dusky color and the description he gives of the sensations he is feeling, we set into motion a predetermined course of treatment to attempt to avert his death. Almost automatically, my partner and I both see our required course clearly.

Evidently having been through this before, the patient protests feebly at the sight of the familiar electrical appliance we are bringing toward his chest. After a brief discussion on the cellular phone, with our corroborators at the hospital, the consensus is that we have to jolt this poor man cold. No sedation.

Knowing what we are about to do is not pleasant, I suggest that his worried wife may not want to watch. She leaves the room apprehensively. The large man lying on the floor confirms that our treatment was delivered successfully with a muffled, agonizing moan as his muscles contract uncontrollably for a split second.

Almost immediately it is apparent that we have caused a dramatic difference in the quality of this man's life. The EKG monitor shows a heart beating normally. He begins to look and sound like a person relieved of a heavy burden. His face reflects his true color now, that of a weathered farmer.

Is he not as heavy as he first appeared, or am I stronger now? We move him onto the stretcher and into the back of the ambulance with little effort. The bumpy nine-mile ride to the hospital is one of uneasy elation. We are all aware that his heart is now susceptible to a relapse, but with the medication he is getting through the intravenous tube in his arm, his chances are getting better with each passing second.

Our friends at the hospital add to our euphoria with praise for a job well done. The look on the faces of the gathering family seems to show a gratitude words cannot express. As we clean our equipment, we go over the details of what we have just accomplished. Sometimes, nothing goes right. This time, everything did. We know we were only doing what any reasonably trained person would have done. The realization that it was not just anybody, but we who stepped between death and this man, gives us strength to go back to the world where the endings are not always so pleasant.

After the short ride back to the fire station, I return to the uncomfortable chair and the book I was sleeping under when the call came. A co-worker asks, "What did you guys do out there?"

With an understatement measured to keep my ego in check, I reply, "Oh, nothing much. Just saved another life, that's all."

. . .

Once we arrived at the scene of a medical emergency just as our ambulance breathed its last. We assessed and treated the sick man in the back of the deceased vehicle while waiting for a replacement to arrive.

An emergency medical technician student, who happened to be the assistant chief of our department, suggested that a couple of us stand on the back bumper, shake the truck, and make the patient inside think that we were on the way to the hospital. Did I mention that the ability to improvise is a very useful talent in this business?

29

DO NOT PASS GO,
DO NOT COLLECT $200

I HAVE HAD THE NOT-SO-DISTINCT HONOR OF BEING A servant of the local incarcerated population for several years. I believe every person has a right to certain human rights, one of which is decent medical care. I do not, however, believe that a hospital should be a haven for unscrupulous persons who are unwilling to pay their debts to society.

Perhaps we have been unnecessarily skeptical whenever being called to the jail. More likely, in my opinion, we have learned to spot actors. Recent history can be very telling in ascertaining a prisoner's true condition.

Case in point: Female arrested four hours ago for driving under the influence. No judge available for arraignment until morning. Has to be at work at 7:00 A.M., or she will be fired. Now experiencing shortness of breath. Thinks her pancreas is about to explode. One time it leaked a little and she almost died. Yeah, right.

One of our best emergency room doctors has coined the phrase *acute thespianism* (roughly translated as sudden onset of dramatic role-playing) for these non-lethal conditions. Many times, when delivering a pre-arrival report to the hospital, we used the term as a significant finding in the examination of the patient dressed in an orange jump suit.

We actually had a young guy tell us that he had a note from his doctor that stated that he should be rushed immediately to an emergency room if his chest began to hurt. The problem was that he forgot the note. It was at home in his other jail outfit, I suppose.

A fellow paramedic has suggested that we write a how-to book, detailing ways to ensure that the restless inmate get a free ride out of the cell and into an emergency room. The problem is, most prospective customers of this kind of literature have spent their last two dollars on a pack of cigarettes just before being arrested. Even if they have the money to buy the book, most are not the type to spend hours reading.

Heart attacks are a great way to get out of jail. The trick is getting the symptoms right: Pain down your left arm, not the right. Pressure in the chest. Not sharp, stabbing pain. The common correct expression is, "It feels like an elephant is sitting on my chest." A little-known affliction of a real myocardial infarction is dull pain in both jaws. Likely, one could get by with pain in only one jaw, depending on what kind of mood we are in.

Sometimes what we do not see is as revealing as what a thirty-year-old athletic shoplifter with chest pain tells us. If one is having a real heart attack, one will sweat. In the blowing snow, a bona-fide heart attack will cause beads of wetness to pop up on the forehead. If you can master the art of diaphoresis on demand, you can write your own ticket to the ER next time you are arrested.

In honesty, we are hard pressed to refuse treatment to anyone who requests our services. Even though we strongly suspect our "patient" is playing us like a violin, we will start an intravenous line with the same size needle we would use on anyone else and deliver him or her to the nearest hospital, at the taxpayer's expense. Anyone who has the intelligence to remember the three magic numbers needed to summon us will get our best effort.

.   .   .

Any time we take someone outside on the stretcher while it is raining, we use a sheet to cover them from head to toe, as a matter of courtesy. Ever the funny guy, I always suggest that the patient raise an arm and wave periodically, so any curious onlookers (or nosy photographers) would know they were still alive.

30

KNOCK, KNOCK

AN EXCITING DIVERSION FOR ME HAS BEEN SERVING
as a tactical paramedic. Some proactive-thinking
police supervisors decided that it would be good to have
someone around to plug the holes if things went south
during a raid. Although the tactical guys typically try to
maintain as much secrecy as possible when they plan a
raid, let's face it: Even the dumbest drug dealer is going
to notice, sooner or later, when a big red and white
ambulance pulls up in front of their crack house. So the
tac-guys just let one of us tag along on their transport.
Guns, ammunition, search warrant, paramedic. Don't
leave home without one.

The tactical unit consists of about a dozen guys who
have passed muster among the most capable police officers. These are men who are very capable of killing,
but just as capable of avoiding doing so unless absolutely necessary. They are trained and equipped for a
myriad of special situations.

Once we were asked to join, we attended some of
their classes. We went to the firing range with them,
and participated in training exercises. At first, there was
an uneasiness between our two factions. Cops have a

totally different makeup than the genteel, fun-loving firefighter. No offense, but most cops are wound a bit tighter than the rest of us. During the first year, we almost always got to play the bad guys in the exercises. They always shot us rather than try to arrest us alive. Slowly, though, we won their hearts over, and they came to see us as the sweethearts that we really are. We became pals, buds. Relatively speaking.

On the routine tactical job, the cops have located some bad guy in town, and want to arrest him. He will be some felon that they think it best to surprise, rather than to have a couple of uniforms just walk up on the porch and knock. We all assemble at Cop Central and go over the game plan. Each officer has a specific job and is to be in a specific place during the entire incident. The idea is to plan well, and to know as much as possible about the site and situation before going in the front door.

Once they are all comfortable with the layout and the strategy, we load into an inconspicuous, unmarked vehicle and drive to the scene. As we approach, the back doors fling open and ninja-looking cops scatter silently in every direction. The lieutenant in charge always drives the van, and I shadow him closely, always keeping him between me and the general direction of the bad guy.

My biggest fear during these exercises is that I will actually have to do something. We always carry a bag loaded with the rudimentary, stop-gap medical supplies. Normally, if time permits, I will ready a bag of intravenous fluid for use as we drive to the scene. I try not to think about the fact that if someone does get shot, every person there is going to turn and look at me. By the grace of God, and the highly competent and professional police officers involved, that has never happened. I guess it does not hurt that most of the bad guys are dumber than a bag of hammers. They never see us coming.

ANNIE, GET YOUR GUN

March 22, 10:44 AM
Medical emergency, 908 Betterduck Drive

We arrive at a well-kept apartment complex and are greeted by an elderly gentleman. As we follow his lead inside, he tells us that his sister-in-law is sick. In the living room we meet an elderly lady. She takes over as guide, and we continue on into the bedroom. There we find an even more elderly, tiny, frail, lady lying on the edge of her bed, but leaning over the side, and clutching a nightstand with both arms.

We quickly realize the lady is blind, or very near. I ask politely what the problem is. "I am holding onto this table so it will stay still. Whenever I let go, it starts moving around," comes the honest reply. "I really feel sick. You people just get out of here and leave me alone."

From out in the hall comes, "Now, Little Sister! You let these nice men take care of you! You need to go the hospital, and find out what's wrong. These people are here to help."

We then begin a ten-minute dialogue with the lady. There are three paramedics among the five of us. We each take our turn trying to persuade the lady to go with us, without success.

Persuasive speech is a fine art that must be learned and constantly practiced. There is an informal game among paramedics that whoever can wheedle the difficult patient into the back of the ambulance, wins. Sometimes the third or fourth debater wins by default, just because the patient is worn down to the point of doing anything it takes just to get rid of us. We are not accustomed to losing these contentions, unless we are just not convicted about taking the person with us.

Suddenly, the little old woman loses all patience with us. "Sister! Bring me that old pistol from the kitchen, so I can shoot these people! They are bothering me, and I don't feel like messing with them. Sister!"

Fortunately, Sister was on our side, and declined to bring the gun. We decided that if the lady did not wish to go to the hospital, we would honor her wish. We thought that better than risking her going to jail for attempted murder (or even murder, if she got off a lucky shot).

We empathized with the younger sister and her husband. We explained that it is kidnapping for us to take a person against their will by force, as long as that person still has both oars in the water. We do suggest that they keep the ammunition really well hidden.

32

A WINTER WONDERLAND

January 12, 9:28 AM
Structure fire, 1100 E. Deepend Street

Today is the sixth consecutive day of below-freezing temperatures. Presently, it is about 10^0F. Rarely does this happen in Texas, and we are not accustomed to taking drastic cold-weather precautions that this requires. Water mains are now beginning to freeze and burst, which imposes somewhat of a problem in a business heavily dependent on flowing water. Without it, we are just so much shiny equipment and guys in heavy clothing.

This is one of the rare occasions when I get to ride an engine. The only reason I get to now is because we are short-handed today, and I am working overtime. Riding an engine and getting paid lots of money. It doesn't get much better than this.

We are snuggled up inside the station when the call comes. It is on the edge of town. Actually, it is outside the city limits. The area is covered by a small volunteer department, and we have a mutual aid agreement with them. It is truly mutual. If they have a fire, we show up and put it out for them. If we have a really big fire, they promise to come and roll hose for us.

The scene is a large collection of apartment-type buildings used as a religious retreat camp by a major protestant denomination, most of whom are southerners. A fairly quiet place, except during schoolbook review time.

We arrive to find an eighteen-unit apartment build-ing heavily involved. It appears that at least ten apart-ments have been consumed, and the volunteers are do-ing little more than following the fire down the line from room to room.

One benefit of having so much fire is that one does not get cold. Whenever I get too far from the source, the water spray begins to freeze on my mustache. It is a moral dilemma. Do I put out the fire and save the prop-erty, or do I accidentally let it continue to burn a while longer, and stay nice and warm? Most people would welcome this much heat today. Being dedicated, and exceptionally moral persons, we do the right thing and go to work.

It is possible to mount just enough defense to prolong the inevitable. If enough water is applied, the fire can be subdued to the point of burning everything in its path, but over a much longer period of time. The water supply out here is inadequate for us to present a winning offense. If we stand in the yard and watch the building burn, it might take an hour to burn completely down. As it turns out, we will spend three hours doing battle in the blistering cold, with the same outcome. We will drive away from a steaming parking lot.

We charge in with two crews and slowly bring the blaze to its knees. Being in a rural area, there are no water hydrants. The best source of water is a swimming pool on the grounds, about two hundred yards away. We place one engine there to draft water out of the pool and into the pump through six hundred feet of hose, and to our other engine on the scene.

After about an hour, we are down to mopping up the remaining hot spots in the destroyed building. Only when our heat source is removed do we realize that it is still cold. It then occurs to us that our engine is still sunbathing next to the pool. It has been sitting there for a while, with no water flowing through the pump. That rookie book-learnin' kicks in, and we all realize at about the same time that unmoving water freezes at 32^0F. When it freezes, it expands.

Sure enough, there is water dripping from beneath the pump. A long crack is visible on the side of the casing. Our inattention has cost the department a sizeable amount of hard-earned tax dollars, but hey! We are warm-weather guys. It never gets this cold in Texas. We will cleave to this dependable logic and promise that it will never happen again.

33

SKINNY DIPPIN'

October 25, 9:45 PM
Motor vehicle accident, 1325 Graywater Lane

We arrive at a location where a major street skirts around a large mobile home park. As part of the aesthetics of the park, the owners have provided a small pond, about a third of an acre. It is about seven feet at the deepest point.

Upon rounding the corner nearest the pool, we can see the top and trunk of a car approximately in the center of the pool. Bystanders tell us they discovered the car, but have not seen anyone who admitted to being the driver, or who was soaked to the bone.

Right behind us is a patrol car with one officer in it. He immediately joins us at the water's edge. He begins pacing the bank, insisting someone has to check inside the vehicle. He is adamant that someone must go in. He seems equally adamant that it not necessarily be himself.

We look around at each other, with every face seeming to say, "Uh-uh, not me. I went in last time, remember?" I do not recall anyone *ever* doing this before, but I know that I have never done it, either. Always seeming to be a sucker for such an opportunity, I hand my empty wallet and my dead man's watch to my partner, take off my shoes, and prepare to wade in.

The ambient temperature is in the upper fifties. Very comfortable. I resolutely set out from shore with my sights on the passenger's door, about forty feet away. The water is probably the same temperature as the air, but not surprisingly, is not comfortable. Once I get over the initial shock and regain my breath (somewhere between my knees and my chest) I lean forward and do something that vaguely resembles swimming the last fifteen feet. I grab the upper edge of the door and reach through the open window. The water is lapping at the top of the opening. Without going completely under. I can grope around inside only into the front passenger's seat.

Knowing that I must search the interior completely, I gulp deeply, close my eyes, and plunge through the window. At the instant I go down, it occurs to me what my purpose is. I am going down in the belief that there might be a body inside. At that same instant, it occurs to me that I really, really hope there won't be anyone there to find. I can imagine few things worse than touching a human body beneath the cold, dirty water in the dark. What if my hand goes into the mouth, or eye, or somewhere else?

I consider lurking just below the surface next to the car, but in a nanosecond my mind indexes through the possible outcomes of that strategy and as quickly rules it out. It would be hard to explain how I could have missed something as big as a body inside a compact car if we towed it out and there were someone inside.

As unpleasant as the prospect is, I crawl through the window and more or less sit down in the passenger's bucket seat. I turn and scan the back seat with my hands. Empty. I feel the stick shift, the dash, the steering wheel, the empty driver's seat.

With a silent "Thank you, Jesus!", I am out in a squish, gasping for breath at the surface, and wading through the sticky mud bottom toward the waiting crowd. Once on solid ground I do not feel like standing around doing a critique of the situation. I insist that my partner drive, and I climb into the back of the ambulance, wrapped in a blanket, and shiver until we get back to the station.

The location is such that on a regular basis we must drive by the little pond. Those who were involved always seem to notice it and recall that night. They never comment on my extraordinary, superhuman courage and grit. They never remark about my commitment to saving others' lives even at great risk to my own health. The only thing they remember is the nature of the water in the swampy little tank. "Look, Nickerson, there's the sewer you went swimming in that night. Ha-ha-*haaaa*." They are only jealous that they did not have the courage to jump in and watch my back.

34

AND THEN THERE WAS ONE

November 22, 9:31 AM
Unconscious person, 1325 Lonesome Highway

We are caught in the middle of our routine morning equipment check. Nothing is worse than to be caught off guard (which seems to be most of the time) and have to rush into something. Without fail, the piece of equipment that you do not check will be the most important device on the ambulance on the next call. Without fail.

I prefer that I have time to drink at least one Diet Dr Pepper before having to do any heavy thinking. I have never been a coffee drinker. The taste is unacceptable to me. You never know whether it will be strong, or weak, or Colombian, or burnt mocha nut. Diet Dr Pepper is the same every time. Oh, sure, every so often, you'll get that one bottle in a million that's all carbonated water. If that happens, you just go back into the store and get a fresh, consistent replacement. Try doing that with coffee. "Gee, the coffee is a tad strong for my liking this morning. You don't mind if I just get a cup out of this other pot, do you? Or better yet, could you just brew a fresh pot, right quick, Big Earl? Thanks. I'll just wait over here."

I gulp down the last three ounces as the tone goes off. We throw everything back into, or at least toward, its place in the ambulance and blast out onto the street. The address is just on the edge of town in one of the many jurisdictional gray areas. It is unclear whether it is inside or outside the city limits. The significance for us is that fire trucks only follow ambulances inside the city limits. Depending on the phase of the moon, and the mood of the dispatcher, we may or may not have an engine crew going with us. This morning, we go alone.

We arrive to find a lady, about seventy, obviously in severe distress. She is barely coherent, sweating profusely, and appears on the brink of unconsciousness. Her husband looks very worried. He tells us that she was not feeling well when she awoke, but insisted on cooking breakfast, as she probably has done for many years. After eating very little, the lady began to feel weak and deposited herself onto the couch, where she is now. She has a past history of heart problems, and takes a long list of related medicines.

By now, having become seasoned veterans, my partner and I quickly recognize the path this person is headed down. It is more like a tunnel, with a bright light at the end.

Reflexively, I reach for her wrist. The pulse is the logical place to start in a situation like this. Even in less urgent cases, it is a good way to look like you know what you are doing.

Without quick intervention she will be gone very soon. Using the most annoyed voice I can manage, I call on the radio for an engine to respond to our location. It, and its crew of three, is at least six minutes away. By that time, we should have most of the technical therapy taken care of, and will be ready to move our patient and all of our stuff to the ambulance.

As we suspect, before we are ready, the lady's heart stops beating. We use the defibrillator to quickly, but temporarily, reverse the condition. Soon she ceases to breathe, and my partner takes over for her. At this point, I am up to my butt in alligators, as one local nurse is fond of saying.

In spite of our frantic yet controlled efforts, our patient's condition continues to slide. By the time the engine arrives, we have completely destroyed the living room of the house with nothing to show for it. We move to the ambulance and continue the fight.

I brace for the roller-coaster ride to the hospital. We follow the well-laid plans of our medical controllers, knowing full well that we are accomplishing nothing.

When we arrived at the house, the lady was still talking, although not carrying the theme of the conversation. From there, it only got worse. Each successive attempt we forced upon her had no effect. She steadily and absolutely died in spite of all our best efforts. God wins another round. With one punch.

It is not a real good way to start off the day. It is easy to feel sorry for ourselves, having been torn out of our comfortable routine. Thrown into chaos so early in the morning. Amidst all this self-pity, we almost entirely

forgot about the woman's husband. We left him standing on the front porch, leaning on his cane. He watched
us do several very unnatural procedures to his wife, and
the last thing he saw was her being taken away with
five big guys hovering over her. We just assumed that
he knew she was dead. By the time we had pulled away,
there were at least two police officers on the scene. It is
their job to take care of the unpleasant interactions with
surviving family members, if we manage to escape without having to do it.

This is a day I will remember.

35

BOY, IT'S HOT! YOU HOT?

August 12, 3:15 PM
Medical Emergency, 1255 Fahrenheit Freeway

During the changing of the guard this morning, the guys we relieved warned us that the collection of assorted nuts and bolts we call an ambulance is having hot flashes. While peering under the hood, and acting like we know what we are looking at (we do this in a lot of situations), my partner and I see nothing to indicate why it would be getting overheated. Like I said, I am a wood-and-nails kind of person on my days off. Metal and hoses make my brain smoke. Having no real conclusive evidence to go on, we opt to keep the thing in service. Maybe it has gotten well overnight. Besides, the reason it is our frontline vehicle is because it is better than the reserve unit. So how would we be helping ourselves by trading a headache for a pain in some lower part of the body?

Our first call is to a nursing home about eleven miles up the highway from our station. About four miles out, little to our surprise, the temperature gauge begins to creep upwards. Not a lot. Not all at once. By the time we are two miles from the address, the gauge is pushing into the red area. Just before arriving, we call and request that a second ambulance be dispatched to our location.

We go about the business of taking care of the patient. He is an elderly gentleman, with typical elderly ailments. Fortunately, he is not in extreme distress, nor in danger of dying in the immediate future. We take care of him, help him onto the stretcher, and move to the ambulance that is taking up space in the parking lot.

With impeccable timing, the reserve ambulance arrives outside the front door just as we do. We grab a few necessities from our original unit and take over the second one. Our cohort is left to baby-sit the hot ambulance until a wrecker can come to remove it from society. It will be dragged back to the city shop. There it will be looked at, much the way my partner and I looked at it earlier today, but with slightly more expertise. Some faulty part will be changed, maybe a thermostat, we will pay our brother city employees an exorbitant amount of money, and the routine will continue.

As we get underway to the hospital, my partner advises me that we may have another problem. Amazingly, this ambulance is overheating also. Because our patient is not in dire straits, we are driving at normal highway speed. The engine coolant slowly loses its battle, and the needle again approaches the red zone.

Being totally frustrated by having to deal with such mechanical malfeasance every day, we decide to run this one until it will run no more. Maybe then we will get something done about this problem. It is hard enough taking care of the sick and dying without having to worry about whether our equipment will get us there and back.

My partner forges on, and is forced to pull over only when the steam boiling up from under the hood is so thick that it is fogging up the windshield. Rather than have a wrecked as well as overheated ambulance, we pull over to wait on yet another replacement.

Our patient is doing okay. He is comfortable, but does not feel at all well. Without the engine, and thus an electrical supply, we have no air conditioning in the back of the ambulance. It is August hot outside, and soon begins to be likewise inside. We ask that the third ambulance come to us as quickly as possible (code three), so the wait will be as short as possible.

After one more transfer, we limp into the emergency room with our sick man. He never complained about the mechanical problems, so we were forced to. Not that it did any good.

The second ambulance will follow the first to the shop. It will get the same cursory treatment and be back out on the street within days, ready to victimize some other poor, unsuspecting crew.

We go back to the station, raise the hood, and start the day all over. Maybe if we had good, dependable equipment we would be invincible. If it ever happens that we get a perfect machine, perfect medicine, and perfect skills, we will put God out of business. But until then, I guess we will just keep fighting and trying.

36

THEY JUST KEEP GOING, AND GOING, AND . . .

May 3, 8:45 PM
Smoke smell, 326 Easter Lane

The engine I am driving arrives at a small house in a quiet, middle-class neighborhood. We are met at the front door by a young lady, probably twenty-five years old. She is strangely dressed, as if she has chosen to remain in the 1960s. She tells us her next-door neighbors have a charcoal grill going on their patio, which is only a few feet from the side of her house. Her worry is not the fire hazard, but that the smoke will harm her babies.

I can barely see her worried eyes behind her cat-eye glasses because the living room is lighted only by a small lamp in one corner. An overpowering smell of rodent slaps me in the face as I enter. While trying to adjust, I notice a small figurine of Ronald Reagan on a small table near the entry. It is arranged within a shrine-like display. I can accept this. Not everyone can be a Democrat.

As we follow her toward the back of the house, we encounter her babies. In the first bedroom, two walls are lined with stacks of small, heavy wire cages. Each cage is about eighteen inches tall, and maybe two feet wide. Inside every cage is a rabbit. Brown rabbits. White rabbits. Brown and white rabbits. At least my perception of rodent hair is confirmed.

The only source of light in this room is a string of tiny clear Christmas lights hanging along the top row of rabbit cages. I then notice that the entire house is dimly lighted, mostly with the same strings of twinkly lights. It gives the place an eerie, ethereal feeling when coupled with dozens of small twitching noses. Were it not for the odor, it would almost be pleasant here amongst all these bunnies.

The lady apologizes for the lack of light in the house, and explains that the rabbits prefer it this way. I wondered how she knew this, but thought it best not to ask. We move on to her bedroom, where there are as many, if not more, caged thumpers staring out at us. Several are arranged around her bed, just allowing access to it, in the event that she wished to sleep.

Outside, we can see the grill smoking. Occasionally, the faint smell of the charcoal can be detected, but it is negligible when weighed against the predominant scent of the house. It appears the barbecue is over. There is no one outside near the grill.

To keep the peace in the menagerie, we assure the lady that we will speak with the neighbors. We further assure her that we do not believe anyone will be harmed by the light smoke. If she is lucky (and how can she not be, with all these rabbit feet?), the tenants next door will limit their cookouts.

After a brief discussion with the people next door, the dispute is resolved. We hop back onto the engine and are soon safely back in our hutch.

37

MAKING THE EASY ONES
LOOK HARD

IT IS PERPLEXING FOR ME TO TRY AND EXPLAIN TO PEO-ple what it is like to work for twenty-four consecutive hours. It looks pretty effortless to get paid for sleeping. It is not necessarily all that easy. Try this exercise at home.

Go about your normal work day. When you get home, sit down and imagine, for a few minutes, that this was the last day at your job: you got fired unexpectedly this afternoon. Now imagine that your house payment is two months past due. Pretend that you went by your girlfriend's on the way home, and she told you she is pregnant. How are you going to explain this to your wife? That should be about the right amount of ambient stress. Now try to relax.

Get four alarm clocks. When you get ready to go to bed (it doesn't matter what time that is), set the clocks. Set one for 2:40 A.M. Set another for 5:25 A.M. Set the third for 7:30 A.M.

Before you get undressed, set the fourth clock for ten minutes from now. This should be enough time to get into bed, and almost become comfortable. When the alarm goes off, jump to your feet and dress as quickly as possible. Run to the garage, fire up the car, and drive at top speed down to the all-night Stop-and-Rob. Go in and buy a can of Vienna sausages for about four dollars. Drive slowly back home as you enjoy your late-night snack. You should be sufficiently awake by now, so go back to bed before the indigestion makes you miserable.

At 2:40 A.M., when the second clock starts buzzing, repeat the process. Note: Be sure you have the alarms set to ear-splitting level. You can skip the supplemental nourishment, if you wish. You may be the type of person who can fall asleep quickly once you are snuggled back into bed. Lucky you.

At 5:25 A.M., same routine. Go! Go! Go! Get dressed as quickly as you can. You can check later to see that everything is buttoned, zipped, and facing the right direction. Ahhh. Smell that fresh morning air. Hear those early birds sing. You should be tired enough, by now, that you are unconscious soon after getting back to the bed.

It is now 7:30 A.M. Time to get up. Maybe take a shower and head for that part-time job. Maybe not. Maybe you can just go home and try to explain to your family how tough it is to have a job where you get paid for sleeping.

38

THIS OLD HOUSE

LIFE INSIDE THE FIRE STATION IS A UNIQUE PHENOM-enon in itself. Each building has its own personality, much as individual residences do. All of them are designed to be virtual homes away from home for three families. These houses each have a kitchen, at least one bathroom, big bedrooms, and a huge garage.

Most of the stations have large, dormitory-style sleeping quarters. This results in five or six mature (at least physically) men sleeping in the same room a matter of feet apart. It is one thing to bunk with your brother when you are a kid at home, but this takes some adjustment of one's thinking.

Until recently we were an exclusive, all-male organization. The rows of beds and one big happy bathroom were not a problem. With the introduction of female firefighters, it was necessary to modify our facilities and our behavior slightly. So we did. Just slightly. It seems to me that we have changed our living quarters more than we have changed our conduct. This will always be a tough place for a woman to work. Not only because fighting fire is a hot, nasty, dangerous job, but because we firemen think we are hot; some of us are nasty, and a few of us are dangerous.

The biggest difference between fire stations and most other domestic dwellings is that each fire station has three separate and distinct families living in it. My family lives there for twenty-four hours, then the out-of-town cousins move in. The next day the three bears take over for a day—when I come in, I look around at who has been eating in my kitchen, sleeping in my bed, and eating my porridge.

Most people wash their dishes after they eat. We usually wash ours *before* we eat out of them. Eating is a major event at the fire station, and we take the entire process very seriously. You could leave a five-dollar bill on the dining room table and it would still be there a week later. You leave a half-eaten cupcake there and it won't last an hour. We have to keep up our strength, you know.

Each shift has its own refrigerator, but that doesn't mean the contents are safe from predators. Usually, by mid-morning, someone has checked the fridge for that leftover lasagna or a big scoop of ice cream. Frustration breeds retribution, so we will spend hours devising some gross response for Goldilocks. Once we iced a cardboard cake and left it out. We carry a drug on the ambulance that we use to reduce a person's fluid load through urination. We were told that milk would dilute its effect to an insignificant level, but no one dares drink from a carton with *Lasix* handwritten on it. Fashioning lick marks, either with a real tongue or by some artificial means, in the top of the ice cream keeps the Blue Bell Homemade Vanilla theft to a minimum.

We play a game of quantum mathematics with our cakes. Once it gets down to the last piece, one is required to take exactly half of the remainder. Depending on the texture of the batter, that last piece can get pretty small. Theoretically, the person eating the last fraction of a fraction of a piece washes the dish. Some unscrupulous guys will forgo their snack and maliciously leave it for the following shift. The problem is, with three crews rotating perpetually, you never catch up to the perpetrators.

In spite of our scheduled duties, extra training, special classes, and an occasional fire safety inspection in the local businesses, twenty-four hours is a long time to stay more or less in one place. With lots of down time, we reach deep within ourselves to calm the pent-up energy, the unconscious fear of having to perform miracles for the public, and the little boy within us. I have played card games and Monopoly, had water gun fights, colored in coloring books, set booby traps, had tennis ball fights, waged volleyball wars, and watched every cable channel transmitted inside our galaxy. Two friends and I actually played hide-and-seek one day. We played for hours, walking around a big station that included offices for our administrative staff. No one really noticed what we were doing. We just walked by and smiled. They just assumed that we were being our usual offbeat, goofy selves.

Firefighters have a lot of quirky habits. We may do things to occupy ourselves during those long Saturday afternoons, but know this: When we turn on that screaming siren, every fiber of our bodies is focused on solving the problem we are being called to alleviate out there on our streets. We all pull together to take care of our customers. So just remember that even under that sad-painted face and bulb nose, Emmett Kelly was a consummate professional on a mission.

FORTY DAYS AND FORTY NIGHTS

March 3, 9:44 PM
Water rescue, 1626 Shoreline Drive

It has been raining for the past two hours. The run-off is quite heavy, intensified by the fact that we have had several soaking rains during the past month. Once the water starts rising, it backs up the inadequate drainage system quickly. Not surprisingly, we are dispatched to a location that always gets somebody when this happens.

A small car was swept into the torrent flowing across a major street and down a concrete-lined channel. Two occupants in the back seat managed to get out before going under. Two in the front did not. The first engine arriving quickly calls for additional help downstream. We are dispatched to a bridge that normally has a brook about six feet wide flowing beneath it. Tonight, the water spans about three hundred feet. We park on the bridge and begin scanning the flowing water with our hand-held spotlight. As the temperature drops and the wind shifts into the north, the rain begins to mix with snow.

After about ten minutes of this agonizing vigil, we hear a crew upstream excitedly describe seeing a girl being swept into a large culvert pipe. She is snared momentarily, but is then gone before they can reach her. From all indications, she is lifeless. My partner and I subconsciously raise our level of awareness as we expect to see the form come beneath our location. Not that we could do much. "Yep, there she comes. That's her, all right. Yep, there she goes."

After fifteen minutes of straining to make out a floating body, we realize that this is going to be fruitless. There is too great a span and we have only one spotlight and a weak flashlight. We radio that we are moving back upstream into town. We will assist in locating the vehicle, which is still missing.

For no cognizant reason, I stop the ambulance atop a small bridge, beneath which flows the channel that the car was originally swept into. We get out just to observe the awesome force the water is exerting on the supports below. As we watch, we see the water is receding rapidly. Suddenly, as I shine the flashlight into the roiling foam, I catch a glimpse of something blue below us. When I look at my partner, it is obvious that he saw the same thing. We fix our gaze back onto the water. Within five minutes the car is plainly visible: It is wrapped almost completely double around the center support of the bridge. I am dumbstruck. Never would I have imagined that flowing water could cause such damage to an automobile.

By now, two more crews have arrived. We anxiously work to get into position so as to determine whether there is anyone still in the car. We dare not risk more lives to locate one already lost. Finally, the water recedes enough to allow us full access to the twisted metal. There is no one inside.

We all agree that searching tonight would be foolhardy. We will return at sunrise. We go back to the station, change into dry clothes, and spend the remainder of the night lying in bed, thinking about the boy and girl still out there in the freezing water.

By morning, the storm has passed. It is clearing and the temperature is a crisp 44^0F. The forecast is for returning clouds bringing two to three inches of snow by nightfall. Our best chance of finding the bodies will be during daylight today.

Our department having no experience whatsoever in body recovery, our leaders begin to organize us as best they can. All those who wish to volunteer may stay and participate in the effort. Always yearning for adventure—and extra money from the overtime—I am among the first in line.

We hurriedly go over a map of the intended search area. We break into groups of three or four and assemble at the designated command post, a short distance upstream from the last sighting.

The media is a step ahead of us. They are waiting near the bridge when we arrive. We ask for a police unit to hold the cameras and microphones at arm's length. This is all new for us, so we expect some blunders as we begin. Even though it is unfamiliar ground, we collectively have a way of adapting, chameleon-style. Our motto in the fire service is "Watch one, do one, and then teach one." In this situation, we are forced to skip to step two.

Each team quickly plunges into the woods lining the creek. Last night the water would have been over our heads in many places where we are now walking. We develop our own system of covering the thick under-brush. The term *helter-skelte*r comes to mind.

By noon, we have covered about a mile of the shoreline. No bodies. We take a lunch break, discuss our tactics, and regroup for another push. One of our wise guys says that he found a body, but it didn't match the description, so he left it. Three guys who are working out of an inflatable raft down the main channel want to set up a gag for the cameras. They propose to stop just out of view of the bridge, get out, and let the raft drift by empty. Hilarious as that would be, our leaders decline to allow it. All afternoon we continue to search without so much as a scare. As night approaches, the temperature drops noticeably and by dusk light snow is falling.

We gather at the station to discuss our strategy. It occurs to me that this is much like a huge Easter egg hunt, with only two prize eggs to be found. I may bring a basket with some plastic grass tomorrow. I also ac-knowledge that I would gladly forfeit all my overtime pay to avoid being the one who makes the discovery.

One morbid fact of water recovery is that a body will float after three days. You search and search for two. On the third day, the victim will come up for air.

About two o'clock on the third day, less than two hundred yards from where the search began, the first drowning fatality is found. The girl is discovered in a place where at least seven people have previously looked.

She is just below the surface, against the bank of the small stream. Within three hours, the boy is found about a mile downstream in much the same fashion as the girl. The grueling search is over. No one is sorry to see it end.

. . .

As cruel as it sounds, I believe in survival of the fittest. Baby birds fall out of their nests for a reason. They are too dumb to make it as grown birds. Anyone who picks them up and puts them back into the nest is doing the bird community a disservice.

I am not saying that all accidents are caused by birds that can't fly. Sure, there are innocent victims, but I have seen a lot of dumb things that caused injury or death to a lot of people. It is our job to pick them up and put them back into the nest. They will grow up to lay eggs of their own.

· **40** ·

EASY FOR YOU TO SAY

March 26, 3:16 PM
Public service, 2601 Phobia Place

We arrive at a two-story apartment building. On the back side, upstairs, is a balcony. On the balcony are a woman and a man. I recognize the woman as a nurse from one of the emergency rooms we frequent. She is a very nice person and has always been friendly to me.

In the discovery segment of this escapade, she tells us that they came outside to enjoy the beautiful afternoon and accidentally locked themselves out of the apartment. They have exhausted everything they know to try. They remained quiet until it was obvious that they could not rescue themselves. He beat on the wall of the adjoining apartment to attract the tenant's attention. The neighbor was kind enough to call us.

It seems like a simple enough job. We whip out our handy short ladder and have it up in a flash. "Okay, Come on down whenever you are ready," I call reassuringly. "Anytime now," I add with cheerful impatience as time passes.

The guy whispers to the woman, who now appears

to be a whiter shade of pale. Finally, he tells us that she is afraid of heights and does not think she can climb down the ladder.

Being the rookie of the engine crew, I am elected to go up and assist the lady in descending the ladder. When I reach the top it is clear that she is petrified. She is shivering uncontrollably and her face is covered with perspiration. I reassure her that we have never lost a life while going down a ten-foot ladder. She is not amused. With me below, and the boyfriend above, we coax her down the short distance to solid ground. Once she reaches the pavement, she relaxes back to a normal person state. She thanks us profusely, and we go about our business of saving lives and property.

About three weeks later, while riding the ambulance, I chance to see her in the emergency room. I say hello and we go about taking care of our patient. Later, while my partner is filling out the dreaded paperwork, she calls me away from the crowd. "I kept waiting for everyone to start teasing me about getting trapped on the balcony, but nobody ever said anything. I just assumed that you would get a big kick out of telling the story. I guess I was wrong. Thanks, Randy."

One thing I am not is insensitive. There are some things that are no one's business, other than those involved. I pride myself in knowing when to keep my mouth shut. I can get all the laughs I need without doing it at someone else's expense.

I guess that makes me a very special person, at least in my own eyes.

41

MONEY CAN'T BUY ME LOVE

July 14, 2:15 PM
Gunshot wound, 2320 Nowill Street

We arrive at a beautifully-kept estate on the edge of town. A man about forty, with tears in his eyes, simply points to a small barn about seventy-five yards away in the middle of an immaculately mown pasture. He already has the gate open, and we drive through.

As we circle around to the open side of a loafing shed, we see a very attractive woman, fortyish, lying completely still on the ground. She is looking straight up, with tears streaming from the corners of her eyes. She says nothing when we begin to ask questions. Through a rapid head-to-toe visual survey, the problem is keenly obvious.

Lying next to her is a blue steel revolver. This sort of clued us in as to which direction to look. Just to the left of midline, below her breast, is a perfectly round hole, precisely the size of a thirty-eight caliber bullet. Our search unfolds outward from there. Now, this is my kind of situation. Something I can put my finger in. We know that she is bleeding inside. We know that we have to try and outstrip the blood loss by replacing fluid.

Upon reaching beneath her back while searching for an exit wound, I discover (the hard way) that she is lying atop a fire ant bed. Following this lead, I discover that she has an almost solid welt from the waistline of her shorts to her neck, front and back. Speeded by the swarm of fire ants, I locate the bullet. It is palpable as a small lump directly beneath the skin, very near the lady's spine. This will account for her lack of reaction to most of the ant bites and the fact that she cannot wiggle her toes.

We have learned well that the most important thing we can do for someone bleeding internally is to get them to a hospital as soon as possible. After brushing away all the ants we can quickly locate, we gingerly move the lady onto a flat backboard. We realize that any movement of the bullet may cause more spinal cord damage than is already evident. It becomes a balance of speed and professional skill. We pay close attention to the technique we use to move the lady, assuring that we minimize the chance of further damage.

Within ten minutes of our arrival we are on the way to the hospital. The woman says very little and avoids all eye contact. I go about my business of starting two intravenous lines and making a more thorough exam of her body to ensure that we have not missed something.

One cannot be too careful. I have this friend (no, not the hosemaster, another guy) who once took a person into the emergency room from a vehicular accident who had an open fracture of the arm. He never discovered it because of the clothing the person was wearing. Not wishing to be embarrassed by a similar incident, I do a thorough search of the lady's body. Fortunately, I find only a few errant fire ants, which I quickly dispatch. As near as I can ascertain in the back of the rumbling, vibrating ambulance, her blood pressure is holding its own against the inevitable leaks with a little help from the Ringer's Lactate.

The bullet entered the lady's chest at the very edge of her sternum (the bone that holds one's ribs together in front). It caught the bottom edge of her bra, and took a perfect half-moon out of the elastic fabric.

Once in the emergency room, the X-rays reveal very little internal damage. The bullet skirted around the outer edge of her chest. But the spinal cord is severed. She will have use of her arms, but not her legs.

All she wanted to do was die. Now she will sit in a wheelchair for the rest of her life. Oh, well. God must have other plans for her. Or maybe He just didn't have a vacancy that day.

· · ·

Then there was the guy who wanted desperately to end it all. He put the nine-millimeter semi-automatic to his right temple and pulled the trigger. The bullet went behind both eyes, severing each optic nerve as it passed. No other severe damage was done. He is still here, but he is now blind. Oh, well. That's pretty final, too.

42

DANG DEFROSTER AIN'T WORKIN'

September 14, 9:12 AM
Injured person, 1515 NASA Drive

We arrive to find a young man about nineteen standing inside the front door of a small apartment, leaning on a bar between the kitchen and dining area. He is bleeding at a fairly good rate, as witnessed by the trail throughout the residence. On the bar is the small, sharp knife he obviously used to inflict the non-lethal cuts to his wrist. Actually, they could become lethal if we just let him bleed for twelve hours or so. Since we have other things to do, we stop the flow and bandage him.

On the way in we passed a young lady sitting in a nearby vehicle, crying her eyes out. As a couple of us begin to persuade the patient that he needs to go to the emergency room for stitches and a talk with the Good Fairy, a couple more of us go back outside to get the girlfriend's side of this drama. After about ten minutes of coercion and half-truths ("You can go to jail for trying to kill yourself!") we have him convinced to take an ambulance ride. The ambulance crew begins the trek toward their vehicle, patient in tow. I pick up the bandage packaging trash and meet a crew member in the front yard.

The paramedic riding the engine with me points out a small car sitting in the parking lot next to the apartment building. On the way in, I noticed that the driver's side window was rolled down about three inches or so. Several old rags were stuffed into the crack. I assumed this was to overcome the effects of a defective window. There is a water hose lying next to the car. It has soaked a large area around and beneath the car.

The distraught girl revealed a scene from this play that the star neglected to mention. She says that following a lengthy argument over the usual love and life issues, the prospective suicide victim proceeded to Plan A. He fed the water hose through the rolled-down window of the car, chinked it with the rags, and turned on the water. He then seated himself inside the vehicle where he full well intended to drown himself. When the water leaked out as fast as the narrow hose could pump it in, he abandoned the car, and went on to Plan B—the tried-and-true wrist slash. Lucky for him, he wasn't much better advised about anatomy than about physics relative to the water capacity of a small, imported car with faulty gaskets.

At the risk of being insensitive . . . okay, I know that I am being insensitive, but this is funny. It would be quite a show to watch a car fill with water and watch a guy drown inside. Not even David Copperfield would attempt something like that. If someone were brave/stupid enough to try it, they would pull quite a crowd.

One would have lots of time to contemplate the past, the present, and the future as a garden hose filled a space as large as a compact car. That last thirty minutes would be agonizing, as your nose is smashed against the top, searching for that last air pocket. It would certainly be a testament to determination.

The human imagination is a wonderful thing. I thought I had seen almost every way imaginable of ending the biological processes that define living. This just shows that I am not nearly so imaginative about such things as I let myself believe.

43

JAILHOUSE ROMANCE

July 14, 7:55 AM
Injured person, 1515 Gomorrah Trail

We arrive at the local long-term lock-up. The guide, a sheriff's department jailer, leads us through the corridors to the scene. He tells us, in very vague terms, that, "This guy has something hanging out under his pants." We quiz him for more information, but he is reluctant to go any further with his assessment of the situation. Something like this could be really good, or really bad.

We are led into one of the large dormitory-style areas. Each dorm has forty-eight bunks, very close together. Each bunk, in a perfect world, contains one inmate.

The patient is lying face down on the concrete floor. He is lying very, very still. Through his loose, scrub-type pants, it is obvious that there is, indeed, something hanging out. The inmates nearby have peculiar looks on their faces. A few are smiling. One looks worried.

Diagnosis: a prolapsed rectum. I heard about it in paramedic school, but this is my first look at one. Imagine reaching into a tube sock, grabbing the toe, and pulling it inside out. You know how it has that sort of fuzzy texture inside? That, as Forrest Gump might observe, is all I have to say about this subject.

The victim speaks no English, but is verbalizing agony in the universal language: "Aye, aye, aye! Aye, aye, aye!" The official story from the inmates is that the guy fell off the top bunk, and this "just happened." Yeah, right! We paramedics pulverize them with skeptical looks. No sense arguing, though.

Suffice it to say, this very rarely happens spontaneously. One must have some help to get it to take place. Since the inmate did not speak English, we were not able to ask any pointed questions.

We delicately load the patient onto the stretcher, face down for obvious reasons of comfort, and to avoid further damage. Medically, this is a very serious condition. The offended tissue is accustomed to being inside a person's body and is now outside, with a very strong muscle strangling it at the inside/outside boundary. This stops the blood flow and if it is not restored quickly, the tissue will die. We drive rapidly and loudly to the hospital.

Upon entering the hospital examination room, the doctor smiles and says, "I wonder what this guy's hobbies are?"

I reply, "We make no judgment about our patients' personal lives, Doc. We just get 'em here alive, if possible."

"Good answer," he says, as he puts on a double pair of gloves.

44

SO I GUESS A MOVIE
IS OUT OF THE QUESTION

October 25, 3:17 PM
Tactical Raid, 3901 Bailbond Blvd.

I am riding along with four heavily-armed tactical cops in a nondescript, unmarked police car, looking out through dark-tinted windows. It is the kind of vehicle you can spot two blocks away, it is so obvious.

We are about to visit a known drug dealer's residence. He lives in a single-wide trailer in a well-kept mobile home park. It is funny how you can't tell by looking at the houses who sells drugs and who doesn't.

This is part of a coordinated raid on several persons related by blood and also by trade. They all sell dope. At two other locations, in other neighborhoods, similar visits are going to take place at the exact moment this guy's doorbell rings—I mean, when his front door bursts into a hundred pieces. This way, no one has time to call Uncle Louie or Cousin Vinnie and warn them.

After waiting a couple of blocks away until all the units are in position, we finally get the green light to hit the bad guy's house. We go squealing to a halt in the street, one door down from the dealer's place. The cops jump out and race toward the house with masks on, guns aimed.

At just the wrong moment, four little boys—nine, maybe ten years old—run along the street in the exact place where the cops need to go to approach the mobile home undetected. They narrowly escape being trampled by the charging officers. Needing something to occupy my time anyway, I corral the four young men, hustle them across the street, and plant them behind the corner of another trailer. This way, I can still see the scene, I am close enough to get there quick, if need be, and I can keep the kids out of harm's way.

To calm us all down, I start making conversation with my new friends. They tell me they are out putting flyers on the doors of all the trailers in their park. The local theater company has hired them to distribute information on the upcoming performance of "The Nutcracker." One of the boys is standing in front of me and I have my arm down the side of his neck, with my hand over his chest. I can feel his tiny heart beating furiously. They are all breathless and chattering incessantly.

Since they had already noticed all the men in black with all the big guns sticking out everywhere, I told them a watered-down version of the truth about what was going on: "The man who lives in that trailer does some bad things, and these police officers are here to take him to jail before he hurts anyone else."

After a pause of probably fifteen seconds, the one I have my hand on says in a very sincere voice, "So I guess there's no use putting one of these things on his door?"

Trying not to laugh, I tell him that he is right. "Might as well not waste one on that guy's house."

. . .

I always got the impression that being emotionally vulnerable was not necessarily a good thing. But after I learned cardiopulmonary resuscitation, it occurred to me that heart compressions would be so much easier if only everyone wore their hearts on their sleeve.

45

BETTER TO HAVE
LOVED AND LOST

January 13, 4:42 PM
Unconscious person, 1325 Lonesome Highway

As soon as we hear the address, we know that it sounds familiar . . . somewhere we have been before. Oh, yeah! This is where the lady died in the living room while we did everything paramedically possible, to no avail. What could the problem be now? We did leave her husband out there. He probably has the flu, or something.

We arrive to find a sheriff's deputy waiting in the front yard. As we begin to get our equipment out, he stops us. "You won't need that stuff," he says bluntly.

The nerve of this guy! Thinks he can tell me how to do my job! Just for that, I carry the LifePak with me anyway, as he turns to lead us around the house.

As soon as we reach the back porch it is obvious that the cop knows more about medicine than I gave him credit for. The widower is lying flat on the porch with his legs hanging off the edge, his feet barely touching the ground. Next to him is a double-barrel, twelve-gauge shotgun. The top half of the man's head, from just above the nose, is splattered on the porch in about an eight-foot radius. Brain, blood, fluid, and bone are scattered everywhere. This is the first time I have seen a body subjected to a point-blank shotgun blast. The base of the skull is visible where the brain normally sits. The jagged edge of the cranium forms a crudely-shaped bowl atop the man's neck.

It takes several minutes for my partner and I to decide what to feel first. Did we somehow contribute to this? After all, his wife died while he watched us laboring to save her. We could have taken a couple of minutes that day at least to acknowledge his presence and explain a little about what was going on. But we were busy.

Why do we have to see crap like this? Deputy Rocket Scientist knew the man was dead. He knew there was nothing even we could do. Why did we have to come out here and see this? It would be bad enough without any prior knowledge of the victim, but this man, especially. What more do they want?

I don't like this job.

46

THE CUSTOMER IS
ALWAYS RIGHT

September 26, 10:18 PM
Medical Emergency, 802 Bull Durham Drive

The call is to assist an elderly gentleman who is having difficulty breathing. We arrive at the door carrying our bag of tricks and an oxygen supply kit. The man appears in his pajamas and slippers. No big surprise. At first glance, in the dimly-lighted foyer, he appears to be a perfectly normal grandfather type. A closer look at his face reveals the first sign that he may be just a bit more off-center than I am.

Extending about an inch downward out of each nostril is something that looks like a white antenna. Wanting to get a little farther into the relationship before asking a bunch of personal, prying questions, we more or less ignore the obvious, for now. We start with the standard questions. "How long has this problem been going on? Does it seem to be confined mostly to your nose? Are you having any pain with this? What are those white things hanging out of your nose?"

He answers as if we were the dumbest dunces he has ever dealt with. "These are pipe cleaners, of course!

They have always worked in the past, but tonight they just aren't working." Well, slap my forehead. Of course! How dense of me not to know about the old pipe cleaner remedy. Why didn't they teach us about this in paramedic school?

We proceed with the routine. Luckily, the oxygen mask is big enough to fit over a nose with pipe cleaner extensions. I wonder if the manufacturers planned for this contingency whey they designed this mask?

We decide to play it coy when we wheel into the emergency room. The nurse who meets us is not fooled for a second. After telling him that our patient is having trouble breathing, he proclaims without missing a beat, "Oh! I see the problem right here. It's these things stuck up his nose." Being less diplomatic than we, he quickly persuades the old gentleman that it is not in his best interest to have a pipe cleaner lodged in each nostril.

We have done our job. We got the man to the hospital alive and no worse off for having been in our care. Since he was moving plenty of air through his mouth, I suppose we did not think it worth getting into a discussion. It would have been just our luck if he had told us that the pipe cleaners were antennae for picking up alien radio transmissions. We have been there before, and have found it better to just let the patient stay in his own comfortable world.

47

LIVE AND LEARN

AFTER IT HAPPENED ABOUT A DOZEN TIMES, IT FI-nally sank in that certain situations can be predicted with some accuracy, based on the initial information given on the radio. When a structure fire is called in as being in the kitchen, more times than not something will be ablaze on the cooktop or in the oven. Seems pretty straightforward, right? With remarkable regularity, the fuel will be beans. Plain old pinto beans, with a chunk of salt pork added for flavor.

I am surprised by how many people cook beans on any given day. It is not so surprising that the occasional absent-minded professor turns on the burner, then runs down to the corner store for a six-pack. The chef runs into an old drinking buddy, gets distracted, then drunk, and forgets all about tonight's entrée back home on the stove, where it is boiling dry. An hour later, the people in the next apartment call 9-1-1. The smoke detector is keeping them awake, and could we please come take the battery out of it?

We bound into action. Fire engines go storming in from all directions, *en force*, expecting (maybe even hoping for) a rolling attic fire in an eight-unit apartment building. The first crew arriving goes clomping up the stairs (it is always upstairs). From two doors away, the unmistakable pungency of pinto beans gone dry is evident. Typically, if we suspect a serious amount of fire is inside, we will break the door open. If we have reason to think that the fire is still confined to the pan and cooktop, we will just break out a pane of glass adjacent to the front door and let ourselves in.

The three-room apartment will be hazy with bean smoke. The cooking vessel, if the bottom is not burned through, will be carried out into the parking lot. The shriveled, barely-recognizable bean char will be dumped on the pavement. We do this as a form of public education for the benefit of the crowd of nearby residents who inevitably will have gathered around the mesmerizing lights on the engines. We should take the opportunity to intone, with severe authority, "This unfortunate young four-quart saucepan lost its life today because of someone's carelessness. Please don't let this happen to your cookware."

We will set up an exhaust fan to clear out most of the smoke from the affected apartment. We can take out the visible haze fairly effectively, but the smell of those beans is going to be there for a long, long time.

It is not always beans abandoned on the stove. Once we found a skillet filled with chicken necks. On one special occasion, we opened the oven door to find a complete cow's head staring back at us through the billowing smoke.

48

SIGN, SIGN, EVERYWHERE A SIGN

WHILE DRIVING AROUND OUR LITTLE COMMUNITY, I realize how many landmarks I can associate with some adventure I have been involved in. Some of the reminders make me smile. Others bring back faces with that cold, gray stare pasted on.

Over there is the House of Rabbits; I wonder how many people drive by this address every day and have no idea that Peter and all his little cottontail friends live there? Up ahead is the half-mile strip of pavement where I have seen four dead bodies on three different occasions. There is the spot where the girl did the nose-dive into the passing lane. Here is where I saw the dead guy who was wearing my watch.

I guess everyone builds a portfolio of memories about the places where they spend their lives. My scrapbook is just a little different than most people's. How many dead and/or mangled bodies do you suppose the town banker has come across in his day's work?

Not everyone marks the miles to work each morning by the ghosts that haunt the roadways. Here is where we helped pick up the lady held together only by her pantyhose. There is the spot where her husband landed.

Sometimes when I am feeling particularly self-indulgent, I thumb through this mental photo album and wonder: How should I look at this sort of thing? Am I overreacting? Am I crazy? Does any of this really matter?

Perhaps I am reading too much into this. Maybe it is no big deal to spend an hour picking up pieces of human tissue along a half-mile of railroad track. Maybe this is the payback for getting to spend the rest of the time on the job being paid for resting.

Maybe I should have gone into banking. If *I* were the town banker, I would sure be making a lot more money. My dreams wouldn't be disturbed by the ghosts of the people I couldn't save. But then, I couldn't look back on those occasions when my being in the right place at the right time made all the difference in somebody's life.

No, I'm in it for the long haul. Some days are longer than others, that's all.

49

MAYDAY! MAYDAY!

February 18, **4:15** PM
Downed aircraft, Middleofnowhere Road

We drive for what seems like hours to reach the far west side of our coverage district. The landscape has gone from urban concrete to wide-open prairie, with knee-high grass and not a tree in sight. From about half a mile away we see the gathering of vehicles, cops, volunteer firefighters, and curiosity seekers. Due to a recent rain, we decide against driving off the gravel road and into the field where the accident has occurred.

We spend a few seconds deciding what equipment we want to lug the hundred and fifty yards across the muddy pasture. There doesn't seem to be much activity at ground zero. This tells us that either the parties involved are pretty much okay, or they are pretty much dead. We prepare for a scenario somewhere near the bad end of the spectrum and begin the trudge across the soft ground.

We can make out the tail of a small, probably two-seat, aircraft sticking into the air. A couple of the local volunteer fire department guys meet us about half way.

"You probably won't be needing that stuff," one offers. I suppress the reaction I reserve for law enforcement officers untrained in emergency medicine . . . but maybe this guy knows what he is talking about. I suddenly recall the old man distraught over his wife's death. Well, better to be prepared for the worst than to get caught without our armor on.

So this is what a small plane crash looks like up close. I have seen countless video clips on the news, but this is my first in-person plane crash. We approach from the rear of the craft, following the same path it took as it plowed into the black soil head-first.

The nose of the plane struck the earth at about a thirty-degree angle. Even though it is a light craft, it dug a two-foot-deep trench about twenty-five feet long before stopping with the nose in the ground with the fixed landing gear still intact, supporting the plane. The windshield and canopy are broken and twisted to one side. In the single seat is the lower half of the lone occupant. His jeans and tennis shoes are still intact, although soaked (and I do mean soaked) with blood. The lap belt is buckled into place just below the pilot's waist. A trail of thick, dark red tissue and blood leads to the upper half of the body. I can smell the muted scent of blood and body organs. The inside of a body has a distinct odor when you unwrap it.

The top half of the man is face down, and has scooped out a trail of topsoil several feet from the plane wreckage. Thank God he is face down. That's all I need— another face to file away with all the deceased persons I have been privileged to stand around and look at while waiting for someone from the coroner's office.

As is everyone on the scene, I am stunned almost into numbness. To imagine the force of impact needed to rend thirty-two inches of flesh and bone completely in two is incredible to me.

Now I know why the six o'clock news never shows close-up footage of high speed, sudden deceleration accidents. Society is not yet quite sick enough to accept graphic images on national television of bodies ripped apart at the waist. It wouldn't take too many shots of a body torn in half before there would be a change in the focus of what people want to see while they eat dinner each evening.

This is why the camera guys wait until the family shows up, and then shove the camera into their faces. That way, we all get to witness their anguish as they experience what is probably the worst day of their lives, and the local station gets their dramatic footage without all that blood.

We lug our useless equipment back to the ambulance after about twenty minutes of close scrutiny. We stay just long enough to capture another of those indelible images that are still so vivid after all these years.

BELIEVE I'LL SKIP LUNCH TODAY

March 22, 9:15 AM
Unconscious person, Secondchance Boulevard

Once we have acknowledged that we are enroute, the dispatcher gives us the additional information she has received from the caller. We are going to assist a man who collapsed while eating breakfast. The caller (his wife) does not believe he is breathing.

We arrive at the same time as the engine crew. We are led into the small breakfast area by a frantic lady. One look at her tells us that this is not going to be good.

Sure enough, the dispatcher was right. The tall, relatively healthy-looking man appears to have taken a dive from his chair onto the floor. He is wedged behind the table, against the wall. Now he is face down, not breathing. It doesn't take a lot of training or experience, to see that this man is dead. What's worse, he coated himself with once-eaten eggs and bits of bacon before he quit breathing.

We spring into action with the routine we have all done too many times before, with too predictable an outcome most of those times. Everything goes fairly smoothly. We get a tube into his airway, past the remains of the Grand Slam, on the first try. The first intravenous line attempt goes like silk. This lets us begin giving the drugs designed to cheat death very soon after arriving. We spend about twenty minutes doing CPR in the house as we prepare him for the move. Once we have him on the stretcher, we quickly go to the ambulance. Three guys pile into the back and continue to pound, probe, poke, and squeeze on the patient as I prepare to drive us to the hospital. On my way around the ambulance to the driver's seat, I reassure the unbelieving family who has followed us out of the house. We always reassure the family. Not that it does any good, sometimes.

Defeat comes all too often when dealing with a heart not working properly. There are so many factors involved that one just never knows what will happen. We go through each step, each procedure, hoping the sick heart will suddenly regain its rhythm, just like on television, but, as I said earlier, what happens is really up to God. It just all depends on what His plans are for the day. I have not yet developed a reliable system for detecting when we will be successful and when we will fall flat on our collective face. Like maybe the person could wink or wiggle a finger when our intervention is working. Nope. They just lie there and stare at the ceiling.

Things go smoothly, and before we leave for the hospital I can hear things coming from the back that sound like we might have a chance with this guy. We begin to get short bursts of beating activity from the man's heart, with an occasional pulse. We adjust our drug intervention accordingly and steam ahead toward the emergency room. Our encouragement is tempered by the fact that we saw this man purple from not breathing about thirty minutes ago.

Past experience tells us that if we are successful in restoring his heart to adequate working order he will have sustained considerable brain damage. Brain cells die pretty quickly without a steady supply of fresh oxygen. He went without air long enough to turn his chest, neck, and head purple. That is not a good sign.

Upon arriving at the hospital, things continue to look hopeful. We pack our considerable stuff, with the patient underneath, into the awaiting emergency room. The ER doctor takes over the orchestration. He extends the therapy we have given to a slightly higher level. The patient continues to hold his own, but like I said, once you have been purple, you seldom remember how to tie your own shoes.

We go about our business. Most of the patient's breakfast is cleaned out of the back of the ambulance. It is always tempting to leave just a little for the oncoming shift, just to show them how bad our day was. As we leave the hospital, the patient is living, but not doing a lot of cerebral interacting with the people around him. We continue to hope that the appointment log on God's cosmic palm-top computer is full today.

51

CAN I GET A WITNESS?

August 4, 2:47 PM

Medical emergency, 1310 Wrongway Drive.

We arrive to find a familiar friend, a young lady about twenty. We have been to her apartment numerous times. Typically, it is late at night when she gets depressed or lonely. About once a month she inflicts non-lethal lacerations on her wrists and forearms. I can never really tell whether she actually thinks about killing herself, or just knows that this will get the attention she apparently needs so desperately.

Today, as we approach the stairs leading up to her apartment, we meet two young men. They are smartly dressed: white shirts, ties, hair neatly groomed. They wear badges identifying them as part of a modern-day evangelical organization. They each have a backpack, though one has laid his aside, next to his bicycle. Both look as if they have seen a ghost, though I am quite certain it was not the Holy Ghost.

The police have arrived about two minutes ahead of us. They spoke with the young salesmen, who very excitedly told of having a one-sided conversation with the patient, and then, all of a sudden, she began to jerk wildly, as if having a seizure. My partner and I turn to look at each other. We say in unison, "Why didn't I think of that?" We suppress the laughter, being ever the consummate professionals.

We go about the routine of treating the young lady as we would anyone whom we suspect of having a clonic-tonic seizure.

After an uneventful trip to the hospital with a girl who appears to have made an amazing recovery in record time, we finish up the paperwork and head back to the station. We realize that we have gained a new-found respect for the EMS system-abusing girl. She has given us a fresh tactic for extracting oneself from awkward, unwanted situations: fake a seizure. More likely than not, your antagonists will not be schooled in neurology. I seriously doubt that they will be back to try and save this girl.

52

I KNEW I FORGOT SOMETHING

April 7, 2:23 PM
Unconscious person, Taxicab Trace

We arrive to find an elderly lady lying on the kitchen floor. She is not breathing and she has no pulse. By now, this scenario has become all too familiar. I am on the engine today, so I begin part of the manual labor part of trying to bring someone back to life. The ambulance guys start an intravenous line in her forearm and intubate the lady.

We go about our job with a sameness that comes from repetition. We go through all the steps without any sign of life from our patient. After about twenty-five minutes or so, we are ready to move to the ambulance. I assist the team in wheeling the lady through the house and out to our emergency room on wheels. As the ambulance crew gets ready to roll, I go back inside the house to tidy up some of the mess we have made. I pick up all the stray needles, a small trash bag full of wrappers from the various drugs and equipment we used.

During the process of trying desperately to save the lady's life, one of her two sons became quite upset. He began to voice his frustration with us and questioned our inability to get his mom back on her feet. We mostly just ignored him, but all of us were a bit unhinged by his behavior. I understand that it would not be a pleasant thing to watch your mother die. That is why we show such restraint when confronted by persons who get unruly.

I finish my job as quickly as possible, and head back outside. The common practice in these situations is for at least one person from the engine crew to ride in the back of the ambulance and help out with the resuscitation efforts. The captain will generally drive the engine by himself out to the hospital and retrieve his help.

Much to my surprise, the engine is nowhere in sight. Both it and the ambulance are turning the corner about four blocks up the street. Here I am standing in the front yard, alone. Well, alone except for the two sons and one daughter-in-law. I am the only one wearing a uniform.

They all look at me, but I can't think of a thing to say. Finally one of the men, the more restrained one, asks, "Do you need a ride?" I can either decline and walk about ten blocks back to the station, or walk two miles to the hospital. It is not my first choice, but I stammer and stutter out a "Yes, I guess so."

Now, this is weird. I have watched dozens of families follow our ambulance to the hospital. Now I am riding in a car with a grief-stricken family, watching the back of the engine as it follows the ambulance through town.

We are not supposed to have to talk to the family after we have failed to save their loved one. We always just gather up our equipment and sneak out while the emergency room staff is dealing with the family. Here I am sitting in the middle of it. Needless to say, the ride was a quiet one. I thanked the family for the ride once we arrived, and went immediately to choke my captain for leaving me standing in the yard. I'll bet that I stay a little closer to the engine from now on.

53

I CAN SEE CLEARLY NOW

September 18, 3:43 PM
Injured person, 1207 Thornbush Way

A police officer meets us in front of the house. His partner is in the back yard with a middle-aged man they found strolling naked through a nearby field of tall grass, weeds, and mesquite trees. The man has numerous scratches from the thorny trees. His left eye is very bloodshot.

One thing about cops: they almost always have the naked people dressed, or at least covered with something, by the time we arrive. They save everything else for us, but at least we don't have to look at a naked guy. When we go around the house, the patient is wearing a pair of cut-off jeans and is sitting placidly on a bench.

We interrogate the apparently unbalanced man, searching for some plausible reason to relay him to the hospital. From what we can glean from this interview, the man believes his eye has offended God, and he should remove it. He tells us that he stuck one of the mesquite thorns in his eye earlier today. He states that he has been antagonizing it with various substances for several days.

The eye is very red, and seems to be irritated, but obviously still functions.

After several minutes of negotiation, we convince the man to go with us to the hospital. He is hard to read and a little bit off track, but appears to be in agreement with what we plan to do. We all walk to the ambulance and assume our positions.

My partner and I situate the patient on the bench in the back and seatbelt him in. My partner takes his seat in the chair at the front of the patient compartment. Everybody is comfy. Now, all we have to do is take a leisurely drive out to the emergency room and pass this tortured soul off to the top of the medical care chain.

I seat myself behind the wheel, adjust the radio to my favorite station, and tell the dispatcher that we are going to the hospital.

It is a beautiful Sunday afternoon. Traffic is light, as one would suspect. My mind drifts to what I could be doing were I not on duty. All of a sudden, a commotion erupts from the back of the ambulance. I feel the weight shift. It feels like they are dancing back there. I hear my partner exclaim in a high-pitched voice, "I need some help back here! Stop that! Sit back down, and put that needle down! I need some help! Now!"

I quickly turn on the flashing lights, pull halfway off the roadway, and set the parking brake. In a tone designed to convey urgency, I request that the police officers who first found this guy come to our location—*now!*

As I yank open the double doors on the back of the ambulance, my partner, who is roughly twice the size of the patient, tumbles toward the opening with a death grip on the man's hand. In that hand, I see an intravenous catheter needle. The guy is squirming, using all his might to free his hand, but he is no match for an excited firefighter.

My partner tells me, in the same excited voice, that the two were calmly enjoying each other's company when, without warning, our guest unbuckled his lap belt, forced his hand down into the plastic needle disposal container on the wall, retrieved the first needle he could grab, and was headed towards his sinful eye, when he was stopped short by the cat-like agility of my partner.

I am trying very cautiously to get an angle on the needle-wielding hand when one of the officers arrives and steps in to clamp the man's fingers. Once he has immobilized the hand, we work together to take the needle.

Now that the honeymoon is over, we have the cop handcuff our patient, place him face down on the stretcher, and strap him down as tight as the seat belts will allow. We then continue on to the emergency room. The mood is much less relaxed and the drive is not nearly so enjoyable as it had begun.

I often think about what would have happened had my able-bodied partner not stopped the guy's hand before it reached his eye. I am convinced the mentally disturbed patient would have gone through with his threat to pluck out his eye. That would not have been a pleasant sight. I also wonder what it was that this guy saw that would warrant so severe a response. When I see something improper, I just turn off the TV.

54

LOVE'S LOST

September 18, 1:48 PM
Motor vehicle accident, 6400 Lost Highway

It is a beautiful day. I am coasting along the route I have traveled a thousand times on my way to work. It is now time to go in and sit around for the rest of the day, sleep all night, get up, and do it all over again.

About five miles out of town I am marveling at the perfect weather. As I am looking across the amber waves of grain, lamenting the lack of majestic purple mountains in this part of the state, I catch something odd out of the corner of my eye. About a quarter of a mile ahead I see an eighteen-wheel tanker-trailer rig veer into the median toward the oncoming lane. The truck goes slowly off the pavement and through the ditch between the lanes. By God's grace, and the fact that his angle of approach took him slowly across the center section, the drivers coming from the opposing direction are able to brake and avoid the behemoth barreling into their paths. The left front wheel of the conventional-style tractor catches a heavy concrete divider that guards an overpass abutment. The truck impacts the wall in such a way that the entire rig rolls up and over in a spiral fashion. It looks just like a television stunt. The trailer stops on its side while the tractor continues to twist until it stops upside down.

By the time the dust has settled, I have pulled to the side of the interstate and stopped parallel to the cab of the truck. For a split second I considered driving on by, but the uniform I am wearing screams, "Stop! Stop!" Okay. Okay. The guy is probably not hurt anyway. I will hang around until the on-duty engine and ambulance show up, and then I can glide on down the road.

As I jog around the rear of the trailer I notice a black goo seeping from a crack in the tank. Liquid asphalt is transported while it is still hot. I can see steam coming from the puddle forming beneath it. This should not be an immediate problem unless it gets on someone. As I approach the cab I can see the driver lying face down beneath where the driver's seat had once been. The top of the cab was torn away as the truck passed over the guardrail upside down. There is, conveniently, about two feet of clearance between the driver and the wreckage hanging above him.

The driver is a big man. I quickly realize that I cannot move him by myself without exaggerating any spinal cord damage he may have. I cannot get close enough to see his face. It appears to be pressed into the soft dirt and grass. I can see enough to know that the front of his head is very bloody. There is no movement. I manage to locate a faint pulse at his wrist. I can detect no air movement within his large chest, nor can I hear any breathing. Without knowledgeable help and equipment, I am just a guy in a uniform. I can stand around and look concerned like everyone else, but there is not much else I can effectively do.

By now a small throng has gathered. There seems to be an imaginary line around the area where the driver lies. No one will get within about eight feet of him, except me. I can because I have on a uniform, with the red patch on the shoulder that says *EMT*. That gives me clearance. Actually, it obligates me.

Even without the uniform I would be going through the same routine. That is what being a firefighter paramedic is all about. We try to help. On duty or off. I now realize that this is who I was born to be. This is what I do.

One woman begins to lecture the driver. "Now, honey, you just hang in there. You will be all right. Just you hang on, hon." I have a feeling he is not going to be all right. Maybe I am wrong, but I don't think so.

Finally, after two eternities, the ambulance and engine arrive. I help carry the equipment over to the site. We carefully roll the man over. My suspicion was right: Honey, you are not going to be all right. Most of his face is gone. We can see his upper teeth, but other than that, no other landmarks are visible on the front of his head. It does not take long to decide that there is nothing we can do. We cover the body with a sheet and begin the trudge back to the ambulance with all the equipment. I turn the whole thing over to my fellow firefighters and finish my scenic drive to the station.

The chain of events and what I saw seem to stay with me longer than usual. I cannot focus on anything meaningful for most of the rest of the afternoon. I finally realize that part of the problem is that I saw something happen that one never expects to see. Not the guy with no face . . . I have seen that before. I am talking about the eighty thousand pounds of eighteen-wheeler crossing the median, flipping upside down, and landing two hundred yards away from me. I only see the aftermath of accidents, not the accident itself.

It is one thing to play with toy trucks when you're a kid, and smash them together. It is different when you see the real thing. It is something that is not supposed to occur. When it does, one's brain has to adjust to rationalize that it actually did happen. Really. I saw it.

Almost four years later, the tracks made in the soft dirt are still visible. The black rubber and metal markings are still very visible on the concrete barrier. It seems that more times than not, when I approach the scene, my mind stops whatever it is thinking about and searches out the ruts in the median, and replays the entire episode frame by frame. I almost reflexively turn to look at the marks on the concrete wall.

The company that owned the truck still runs along the highway on a regular basis. Like all the other drivers on the road, I see their logo on their tankers. Unlike all the other drivers, I can see the logo upside-down, the entire vehicle in mid-air, doing a snap roll onto its side. I never pass the place without seeing that truck, smelling the spilled asphalt, and, oh yeah, seeing the driver wearing a red plaid flannel shirt, with his face missing.

55

BELIEVE I'LL HAVE
ANOTHER SANDWICH

October 12, 12:07 PM
Not just another day at the office.

Once a year, during "National Love Your Local Fire Guys Week," one of the local hospitals hosts a luncheon for us. We get to go by and eat a delicious, fattening, and cholesterol-laden lunch outside the emergency room. Seems a bit ironic, doesn't it? It is always nice to know that what we do is appreciated.

On this particular occasion we get a special surprise. When we arrive, a tall man, probably fifty, greets us. I don't recognize him at first. I assume that we helped him or one of his loved ones out of a bind sometime in the past. As we mill around waiting for the meal to begin, word circulates that this is the man who collapsed behind the table one morning at breakfast.

No way! That guy was dead! We got his heart working again, but there is no way that he didn't have massive brain damage. I guess it's possible . . . but he looks so different without all that scrambled egg and bacon on his shirt.

As we eat together, the man talks of life as if he sees something different than we do. He certainly seems to enjoy his meal. How strange it must be to have been, by our definition, dead. I cannot begin to imagine. Would I change my priorities if I got to peek over that hill? Would food taste better? Would I not take my family for granted so often? How many of us will get the opportunity that this man was given?

This is the reason we do what we do. We save lives. There is no doubt whatsoever that this man would absolutely be in a casket six feet under today had we not intervened on that fateful day. This makes our service worth every tax dollar. It only takes one life to pay the bill.

The man gave us a small certificate that says, "Thanks for saving my life!" It sounds so strange when I read it. People get credited with saving lives, but we have documentation.

I have to admit it. I love this job.

· 56 ·

AS THE CURTAIN COMES DOWN

WHEN I BEGAN THIS ADVENTURE, I WAS YOUNG AND wide-eyed. I began with a fair amount of trepidation about the whole profession. As I learned, and watched, and performed the skills, I slowly became comfortable wearing this responsibility.

It has been such a gradual process that I cannot look back and mark the day when I knew I was truly a professional firefighter. It just evolved.

After spending almost half my life doing it, this job still intimidates me a little. There is always the thought in the back of my mind that says, "What if I can't do it? What if I mess up, and someone gets hurt? What if we fail someone who calls us?" That fear is what gives us an edge. We always concentrate just a little bit harder, knowing that everyone is watching. When someone dials or punches or otherwise calls 9-1-1, they are counting on us. That's okay. We will handle it.

The Denton Fire Department has served me well, and has given me a lot of memories.

Thanks for reading.

ADDENDUM:
MERELY A TECHNICALITY

OVER THE YEARS WE HAVE PUT TOGETHER SEVERAL special units within the fire department under the broader scope of emergency management. We have had hazardous material (Haz-Mat) teams, swift water rescue teams, urban search and rescue specialists, and others. Typically, we will start out like gangbusters, then interest gradually fades. All the expensive equipment will end up back in a corner gathering dust. If ever the need arises, we will be there in a flash, but for the most part, the entire department handles any disaster—not just a few with individualized training.

Not always, but at times, these start-up groups will be driven by some incident in or around town or in the news. If a space shuttle were to crash west of town we would probably buy rocket fuel removal equipment.

One day we came in and found a new memo on the bulletin board. A new technical rescue team was being formed. We are looking for a few good men. It gave examples of skills and certifications that would be helpful to team members. This one was different in that prospective team members were asked to fill out a sort of application. The people in charge would decide who would be on the team. At least that was the impression we got at my station.

This ruffled our feathers a bit. The nerve of these guys! If we want to be on a technical rescue team, we will start our own! As fate would have it, we had recently had a spectacular train crash in the middle of town. Miraculously, no one was seriously injured; it just made a mess. One thing led to another, and before the day was over we had put together an application for our own team of elite technical train rescue storm troopers. We put the application in all the stations. We didn't get any serious applications, but we did return the favor of ruffled feathers. They knew we were turning the spotlight back on them, but they could find no way to quiet the laughter long enough to rebut our little prank.

This is what the Technical Train Rescue Team Application looked like:

Re: Technical Train Rescue Team

As the *Denton Record-Chronicle* reported, there have been at least three recent, notable train wrecks in Denton. The first was in 1939. Disaster struck again in 1965, and, most recently, in 1996. We feel we must begin to prepare ourselves now if we are to be ready for what appears to be a pattern of major train events occurring every twenty-seven years or so.

It is incumbent upon the Fire Department to implement a Technical Train Rescue Team, and to furnish the resources to achieve the desired results. To this end we are committed to put our department on track (so to speak) in order that we might meet our objectives.

The recently formed Technical Train Rescue Team proposes to raise our department to the pinnacle of railroad mishap management. We propose to transform our members into finely-tuned, sharply-honed machines. This assignment will not be for everyone. Therefore we will diligently screen each aspiring member (see attached application).

We will invest enough time doing train stuff that the exorbitant amount of money we spend will begin to seem almost legitimate.

We will attempt to produce from Union Pacific two hand-driven cars, to be used strictly as rescue and recovery vehicles. Every member will be trained in how to propel the vehicle by using an up and down motion. Each Certified Technical Hand Pumper will be required to recertify every six months to ensure our proficiency in hand car rescue.

We will seek permission from the owners of Harpool Garden Center to use their anchored antique caboose for frequent training sessions.

We will procure and maintain a complete collection of Boxcar Willie CDs.

In order that our elite team members will be easily distinguished from your average, untechnically-skilled firefighter, we will provide at least one pair of striped overalls for each member.

We will make every attempt to avoid making the rest of the Fire Department look woefully inadequate in their feeble attempts to do their jobs, all the while knowing that we are head and shoulders above the average, garden variety firefighter.

Disclaimer: Any similarity to actual organizations, events or persons may not be entirely unintentional. No real attempt was made to avoid such a coincidence. So sue us.

— —

Denton Fire Department
Technical Train Rescue Team
Serving Denton's Railroads Since Mid-1996 or So
"We're Loco-Motivated to Train"

Application for Membership

Name: _____

Station (Fire, not Train): _____

To be on the team, you do not need any specialized training, just the desire to act as if you are specially trained. List below if you do have any specialized training or skills such as: having been to the Forest Park Zoo and riding the train there; ticket taking, swinging a lantern, knowing how to tell time on a pocket watch; having ever put a penny on a railroad track to see how flat it will be after a train runs over it; knowing what creosote smells like, having once lined a flowerbed with crossties; and/or knowing the difference between a coal tender and a chicken tender. If, as a kid, you ever threw rocks at a locomotive or owned a Lionel train set; or, if you have ever drunk spiked punch, worn spike heels, seen a Spike Lee movie, or had a dog named Spike; or, if you ever heard a tornado and thought it was a train, these are all admirable attributes that will make you look like a really technical kind of rescue guy.

Please include the date of your very first train sighting, and any pictures of trains you may have.

ABOUT THE AUTHOR

CAPTAIN RANDY NICKERSON has served the City of Denton, Texas, as a firefighter paramedic since 1979. He is a graduate of the University of North Texas (Bachelor of Science, Education) and the University of Texas Health Science Center Medical School paramedic program, which was developed for the Dallas Fire Department.

While taking a literature course at North Central Texas College, Randy wrote an essay related to an ambulance incident as a class assignment (see chapter 28, "Life Goes On.") His instructor, Linda Coolen, entered the paper in a literary contest. To Randy's utter amazement, he won the contest! Encouraged by his mentor and friend, Dr. George Christy, he began writing down more of his memorable career experiences. The result is this book.

After more than twenty years in the fire service, Randy's chief responsibilities now are supervisory, but he is still called frequently into hands-on service. Randy and his wife, Ava, reside in Valley View, Texas. They have two sons, Joel and Jordan.

Printed in the United States
73598LV00001B/1-99